management and control

Tutorial

Michael Fardon

osborne
BOOKS

Published by Osborne Books Limited
Unit 1B Everoak Estate
Bromyard Road
Worcester WR2 5HP
Tel 01905 748071
Email books@osbornebooks.co.uk
Website www.osbornebooks.co.uk

Design by Laura Ingham
Cover and page design image © Istockphoto.com/Petrovich9

Printed by CPI Antony Rowe Limited, Chippenham

British Library Cataloguing in Publication Data
A catalogue record for this book is available from the British Library

ISBN 978 1905777 396

Contents

Acknowledgements

The publisher wishes to thank the following for their help with the reading and production of the book: Mike Gilbert and Cathy Turner. Thanks are also due to Roger Petheram for his technical editing and to Laura Ingham for her designs for this new series.

The publisher is indebted to the Association of Accounting Technicians for its help and advice to our authors and editors during the preparation of this text, and also for allowing the reproduction of its sample assessment material, included at the end of this book.

Author

Michael Fardon has extensive teaching experience of a wide range of banking, business and accountancy courses at Worcester College of Technology. He now specialises in writing business and financial texts and is General Editor at Osborne Books. He is also an educational consultant and has worked extensively in the areas of vocational business curriculum development.

Introduction

what this book covers

This book has been written specifically to cover the Learning Area 'Credit management and control' which covers two QCF Units in the AAT Level 4 Diploma in Accounting:

- Principles of Credit Management
- Control of Debt and Credit

The book contains a clear text with worked examples and case studies, chapter summaries and key terms to help with revision. Each chapter has a wide range of student activities.

AAT Sample Assessment

This tutorial text also contains a sample project assessment produced by the AAT, together with AAT's guidance answers. This should help students familiarise themselves with what is required for their computer-based assessment and online project-based assessment.

International Accounting Standards (IAS) terminology

In this book the terms set out below are quoted as follows when they first appear in a chapter (and elsewhere where it seems appropriate): IAS terminology (UK terminology), ie

receivables or trade receivables (debtors)

receivables analysis (aged debtors analysis)

payables or trade payables (creditors)

inventory (stock)

non-current assets (fixed assets)

revenue or sales revenue (sales)

profit from operations (operating profit)

income statement (profit and loss account)

statement of financial position (balance sheet

IAS terminology is therefore generally used throughout this book, except where the term is quoted in a legal context, eg 'debtor' and 'creditor' in insolvency proceedings.

1 Introduction to credit control

this chapter covers...

Credit control is the process of managing customers who pay on credit so that settlement of debt is made on time.

Efficient credit control is essential for maintaining the liquidity of an organisation; money not received may mean that money will have to be borrowed.

This chapter starts with an overview of the whole credit control process – from credit application to debt collection.

The chapter then concentrates on the ways in which an organisation obtains information which enables them to assess the suitability of:

- customers who are applying to trade on credit terms

- existing customers who have already been granted credit terms

This assessment process involves:

- examining the external sources of information – for example, banks, credit rating agencies and other suppliers

- examining the internal sources of information available to help with the assessment decision – reports from colleagues (eg sales records, notes on visits) and analysis of financial accounts

The next chapter describes in detail how a customer is assessed by means of credit analysis of financial accounts made available to the supplier. This will involve the calculation of performance ratios and the application of a credit scoring system.

LIQUIDITY AND CREDIT CONTROL

the importance of liquidity

Liquidity is a measure of the extent to which a person or organisation has cash – or can raise cash – to meet immediate and short-term liabilities.

As you will know from your studies of cash management, **liquidity management** in an organisation involves the **timing** of cash inflows and outflows – including financing and investing – so that the organisation has sufficient working capital and remains solvent.

The main sources of liquidity are – in order of liquidity – cash, bank deposits, receivables (debtors), inventory (stock). This book concentrates on the management of **receivables (debtors)** through efficient credit control – the granting of credit, the monitoring of customer accounts and effective collection of debts.

Of course, the need for liquidity management will vary according to the nature of the organisation. For example, businesses such as shops, operate on the basis of **cash sales** and do not run the same **risks** as the business that relies to a greater extent on credit sales – ie buy now and pay later.

external methods of improving liquidity

You should note that there are a number of financial services available to organisations which can help them with debt collection and the avoidance of bad debts. These services are provided by banks, insurance and other financial institutions. They will improve or safeguard the liquidity of the organisation, but at a cost. They include:

- **credit insurance** – insuring against the risk of non-payment, both in the UK and overseas – accounts covered can be single customer accounts, key accounts, or general coverage
- **factoring** – a factoring company lends money against the invoices received from receivables (debtors) of the business, providing liquidity before the invoice due dates; the factoring company actually takes over and runs the sales ledger
- **invoice discounting** – a finance company lends money against invoices issued to selected customers of the business, but the business continues to operate its own sales ledger and credit management system so that the customer does not realise that the finance company is involved

There is more information about these schemes in Chapter 5, pages 89-90.

THE CREDIT CONTROL FUNCTION – AN OVERVIEW

Credit control is the process of managing customers who pay on credit so that settlement of debt is made on time.

An important element of liquidity management is the efficient functioning of the sales ledger – or in basic terms, customers paying up on time. If customers do not pay up on time, or – worse still – become insolvent, this can be the result of:

- credit terms being granted to customers who are not creditworthy (a failure in the system when the customer applied for credit), or
- the payments of the customer not being monitored effectively and warning signs of customer financial problems not being picked up (a failure of the sales ledger management system)

The result is likely to be the same: a bad debt and a consequent loss of profit.

Credit control forms part of the accounting and finance function of an organisation. The number of people employed in credit control will depend on the size of the organisation. It may be a whole department, a section, or in the case of a small business, the accounts assistant or even the proprietor. The credit control activities carried out are summarised in the diagram on the next page, which you should study carefully. They include:

- assessing new applications for credit (either from new customers or from existing customers looking for an increased credit limit)
- monitoring sales ledger accounts by using reports such as the receivables (aged debtors) summary
- chasing overdue debts and dealing with bad debts

Larger organisations are likely to have a **credit control policy**, a written set of procedures detailing issues such as assessment methods, credit terms granted, chasing of debts, and dealing with bad debts. An example is shown on page 14. It will normally be accompanied by documentation such as credit application forms, sales contracts and chaser letters.

People who work in credit control need to be highly experienced in communication skills: they are negotiators and persuaders, but should also be able to take on the role of rotweillers.

the credit control process

The diagram on the opposite page illustrates all the stages involved in the credit control process. This chapter concentrates on the external and internal sources of information that can be used to reach a decision on whether or not to grant credit terms to a customer. This area of study forms the top part of the diagram, shown inside the dotted line box.

the credit control process

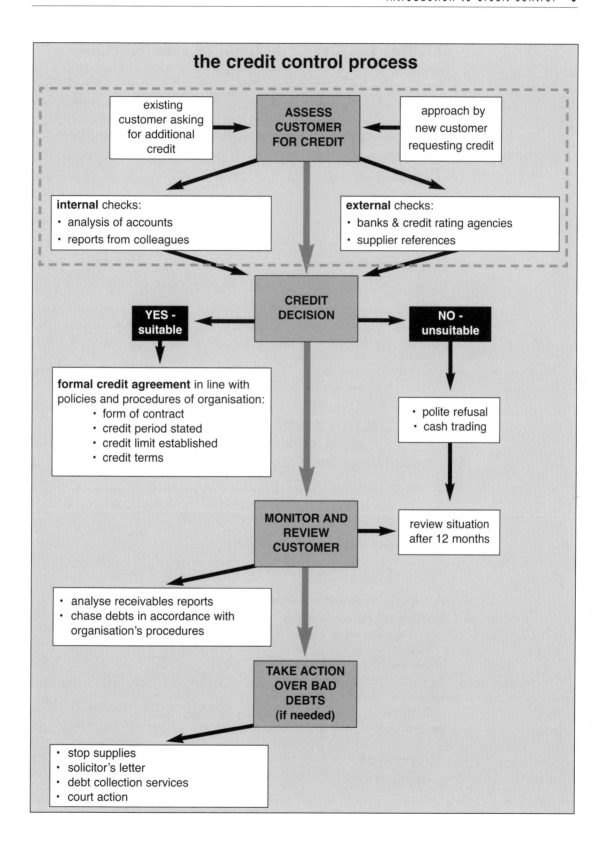

EXTERNAL SOURCES OF INFORMATION ABOUT CUSTOMERS

using sources of information

Organisations can consult a variety of sources of external information:

- bank references
- supplier (trade) references
- credit circles
- credit rating agencies
- accounts filed at Companies House
- official publications
- management accounts – but obviously only if they are made available

The credit control policy document of the organisation (see page 14) is likely to provide guidance about establishing the creditworthiness of a new customer and indicate what external sources should be approached.

Obviously common sense tells you that the size and importance of the customer will dictate what checks will need to be made. If you are a wholesaler supplying a supermarket you are likely to use different checks than you would if you were supplying a corner shop.

It is common practice for an organisation to send out a letter to a new customer along the lines of the following:

Dear Sirs

Ref : Application to Open a Credit Account

Thank you for your request to open a credit account in our books.

So that I can consider your request I shall be grateful if you will supply me with:
- details of your bank account - bank, bank branch address and account name, plus your written authority to your bank to release information
- details (contact names, addresses, telephone numbers) of two trade references

Thank you.

Yours faithfully

Conrad Troll
Credit Control

Alternatively, the organisation may have a credit application form which it sends to customers applying for a credit account. Details might include :

- the registered name and address of a limited company, or
- the names, business and home addresses of partners, or
- the name, business and home address of a sole proprietor
- the length of time they have been in business
- any trading name used
- at least two trade references
- bank details, plus an authorisation to obtain a bank reference
- credit requirement
- signature of the applicant(s)

An example is shown below.

APPLICATION FOR CREDIT

Please open a credit account in the name of ....

Address ....

....

Telephone.. ....Years in business...............................

Trading name(s) where applicable ....

Amount of credit required £ .... monthly, in total £ ....

Please accept this as authority to release information to the parties below for reference purposes.

signed .... capacity .... date.........................

signed .... capacity .... date.........................

Bank name..

Bank address...

Trade reference 1	Trade reference 2
Name...	Name...
Address	Address ....
....	....
....	....
Tel..	Tel..

bank references

Banks have traditionally been a valuable source of information about the credit standing of prospective customers.

One problem with bank references is the language in which they are written. Banks are experts at understatement. Just as school reports need interpretation – eg 'she is a quiet student' means 'she is asleep most of the time' or 'she is lively in class' means 'she talks incessantly' – so bank reports also need interpretation.

A request for a bank reference is normally worded along the lines of:

'Do you consider Dodgee Builders Limited to be good for the figure of £50,000 trade credit per month?'

The replies that might be received are shown below, both in bank language and also in plain ordinary English. The replies are listed from top to bottom in order of creditworthiness.

bank reply	plain ordinary English
'Undoubted.'	'A good risk for the figure quoted.'
'Good for your figure and purpose.'	'A reasonable risk and most probably OK.'
'Should prove good for your figures and purpose.'	'Not so sure about this one - well worth investigating further before making a decision.'
'Although their capital is fully employed we do not consider the directors would enter into a commitment they could not see their way to fulfil.'	'This business has cash flow problems and should not be allowed any credit.'

When translated into plain English, bank references are limited but useful indicators of the prospective customer's creditworthiness.

trade references

It is common practice for organisations to ask for two trade references when assessing a customer's credit risk. These are not always reliable because the prospective customer might give as references suppliers who are not strict about credit control, and avoid quoting the suppliers who are red hot in chasing debts.

A standard letter asking for information from a trade referee is shown below.

Fine Dowt Limited

88 Station Road
Newtown NT6 9GH
Tel 01707 767188 Fax 01707 767022 www.finedowt.co.uk

Credit Control Manager
Esloy Engineering
Unit 16 Forest Estate
Bath BA2 4JP

We have received a request for credit from our customer Parsons Printers. They have quoted you as referee. We shall be grateful if you could answer the following questions.

How long have you been trading with the customer?   ....years .... months

Terms granted   amount per month   £....................

Total limit   £...

Period of credit granted   ....

Payment record (please indicate as appropriate)   prompt / occasionally late / often late

Have you ever suspended credit?   Yes / No   When?...............................

Other relevant information ....

....

Thank you for your assistance. We will be happy to reciprocate at any time.

Yours faithfully

N Igmer

Nigel Igmer
Credit Controller

A reply to a trade reference may take a long time to process. The enquiring organisation can avoid delay by telephoning the enquiry to the 'sales ledger' staff after sending off the credit enquiry letter.

credit circles

An alternative adopted by some businesses is not to make the trade enquiry through the quoted referees but to telephone one of their own competitors (who are likely to deal with the customer) and speak to the sales ledger staff directly and informally – often receiving a very honest appraisal. This slightly practice is sometimes known as a **credit circle**, ie a group of businesses in the same trade who exchange information about customers they have in common, and particularly those who may be experiencing cash flow problems.

credit reference agencies

Organisations which frequently process new applications for credit often subscribe to **credit reference agencies**. These are commercial organisations which offer an on-line service for checking the credit rating of companies and individuals. They have extensive databases which provide a wealth of material which can be provided on demand, enabling an instant credit decision to be made. They do, of course, charge for the service, and there is the risk that some of the information may be out of date. Examples include:

- **Dun & Bradstreet** (www.dnb.com)
- **Experian** (www.experian.co.uk)
- **Equifax** (www.equifax.co.uk)

Reference enquiries can be made either on limited companies or on individuals.

Reports from credit reference agencies on **limited companies** will provide details such as:

- three years' accounts
- payment history
- directors details
- any insolvency proceedings

Credit reference agencies are widely used for providing reports on **individuals** for organisations such as banks, credit card and hire purchase companies. Sole trader and partnership businesses are enterprises run by individuals. These reports will not produce much in the way of financial data (only limited companies have to file their accounts) but will provide information such as:

- names and addresses
- credit risk – based on any default on credit (including not paying credit card bills on time)
- county court judgements for non-payment of debt
- bankruptcy orders

Reports on individuals can be requested to check up on the credit rating of directors of limited company customers. A director with a bad credit record can often be found to be running a company which is also a poor credit risk.

Companies House

Another source of information about limited companies is Companies House, the Government agency to which all larger limited companies are obliged by law to send their annual accounts and to which all companies send information about directors (www.companieshouse.gov.uk).

This data is publicly available (at a cost), but financial data may not be completely up-to-date, as many companies file accounts well after the balance sheet date.

other published sources

If a credit control department wishes to find out about the creditworthiness of a large organisation it may find references and articles in the press, trade journals and online. The internet is a powerful tool here. Try doing a search on a well-known company name in www.google.co.uk, for example, and see what information and up-to-date news articles are produced.

management accounts

An important element of the assessment of the customer risk is analysis of the customer's **management accounts**, if they are available. This will involve the use of **performance indicators** to analyse past and up-to-date financial statements of the customer. If up-to-date financial statements are not available, draft accounts or internal management reports should be requested for analysis. Ideally, at least three years' accounts should be analysed in order to show the trends in three key areas:

- **liquidity** – the ability of the business to repay debts as they fall due
- **profitability** – the ability of the business to maintain its capital and to provide funds for repayment of debts in the future
- **gearing** – the financial risk taken on by the business shown by comparing interest bearing liabilities and total capital employed

This area of assessment and the use of **credit scoring** are covered in full in the next chapter.

A NOTE ON THE DATA PROTECTION ACT, 1998

When an organisation asks for a reference from a company, bank or credit reference agency, it is asking that organisation to disclose data it holds which relates to a third party (someone else). The law is very strict on this point as there is a real danger that the information may be incorrect or the person or organisation to which it relates does not want it to be released.

The current legislation covering this area is the Data Protection Act 1998, which has reinforced existing rules for the processing of personal data. It follows the guidelines of a European Directive and brings the UK in line with European legal principles. The Act applies to:

- data about individuals (eg sole traders, partners) but not about companies

- records held on computer – eg a computer database of names, addresses, telephone numbers, sales details of each customer ('data subject')

- manual records – eg a card index file system of customers details

All organisations which process personal data should register with the Data Protection Commission and should follow the eight guiding principles set out in the Data Protection Act. These principles require that personal data is handled properly. They state that personal data must be:

1 fairly and lawfully processed

2 processed for limited purposes

3 adequate, relevant and not excessive

4 accurate

5 not kept for longer than is necessary

6 processed in line with the data subject's rights

7 kept securely

8 not transferred to countries outside the European Union unless it is adequately protected in those countries

Individuals have the legal right to know what personal details about them are held by an organisation such as a credit reference agency. They should apply in writing to that organisation for a copy of the personal data held on file; they are likely to have to pay a small fee for this service.

INTERNAL SOURCES OF INFORMATION ABOUT CUSTOMERS

External sources of information are often used when the individual or organisation applying for credit is not known to the enquirer. If an organisation needs to assess the credit risk of an existing customer – eg when an increase in credit limit is requested – much of the information needed may already be available within the organisation. This **internal** information includes:

- internal conversations and emails
- records of meetings and visits by employees of the organisation – eg by sales ledger and sales teams

internal records

Suppose two existing company customers (A and B), each with a credit limit of £10,000 ask for an increase to £15,000 because of increased trading. The credit control staff could make enquiries within the organisation . . .

Company A: Go-A-Head Limited	Company B: Going-to-the-Wall Limited
feedback from sales ledger team	**feedback from sales ledger team**
'Yes, they always pay on time. Never go over their limit. No problems there.'	'Not sure. They always seem to be up to their limit or slightly over. The money comes in, but it is often late, and we have had to send out chasers.'
feedback from the sales team	**feedback from the sales team**
'Yes, we went to see them last month. They seem well-organised and there is a good market for their product. They are well positioned for expansion. They find our prices very competitive. They are good to do business with.'	'We asked to visit them, but they didn't seem keen. They have a high turnover of staff – we always seem to be dealing with someone different. I personally think that they have been over-ordering from us as I am not sure that their sales are up to target. I wonder if they need the higher limit to help fund their liquidity?'
conclusion of credit control team	**conclusion of credit control team**
'On the face of it a good credit risk, but we will need to see their accounts.'	'There appear to be problems here, so we will need to see their accounts. We may struggle to recover what is owed!'

THE ORGANISATION'S CREDIT CONTROL PROCEDURES

It is important to appreciate that the credit assessments explained in the text of this chapter are likely to form part of the organisation's credit control procedures, often set down in a formal written policy document.

Where there is such a document, there will be operational requirements, set terms, standard documents, all of which will ensure that the administration of credit control runs smoothly and in line with the organisation's 'standard' procedures.

Another reason that standard procedures have to be followed is a legal one. The relationship between seller and buyer is one of contract, ie legal agreement.

If that contract is broken – eg the buyer does not pay up – the seller may need to take the buyer to court. The law is very particular and if the seller is to be successful, it is very important that all the procedures have been carried out 'to the letter'. This is particularly important in relation to terms of payment. This issue will be dealt with in full in Chapter 6.

Set out below is an example of a typical Credit Control Policy Document. Note that the Sales Department – who will be dealing with the customer on a day-to-day basis – will need to be notified of any default procedures.

CREDIT POLICY & PROCEDURES

New Accounts	1	One bank reference and two trade references required.
	2	Analysis of minimum of three years' accounts for limited company customers.
Credit Terms	3	Standard terms 30 days from invoice. Any extension to be authorised by Credit Controller.
	4	2.5% settlement discount at Credit Controller's discretion.
Debt Collection	5	Invoices despatched on day of issue.
	6	Statements despatched first week of the month.
	7	Receivables analysis produced and analysed first week of the month.
	8	Reminder letter sent first week of the month for accounts 30 days overdue (Letter 1).
	9	Telephone chaser for accounts 45 days overdue. Meeting arranged if required.
	10	Customer on stop list if no payment received within 15 days of telephone chaser (unless meeting arranged). Sales Department notified.
	11	Letter threatening legal action and stop list notification sent if payment not received within 30 days of first letter (Letter 2).
	12	Legal proceedings set in motion if payment not received within 30 days of Letter 2 – subject to authorisation by Finance Director and notification of Sales Manager.

Chapter Summary

■ Sufficient liquidity in an organisation – its ability to meet immediate liabilities – is critically important because it will help to ensure that it remains solvent.

■ An effective credit control policy is essential in an organisation if liquidity is to be maintained. The prompt receipt of payments from receivables and the avoidance of bad debts are its key objectives.

■ The extent of the credit control function depends on the size of the organisation. The same basic functions will be carried out:
  • assessing applications for new credit from new customers
  • assessing applications for increased credit from existing customers
  • monitoring the sales ledger
  • chasing overdue debts
  • dealing with bad debts

■ Organisations use a variety of external sources and internal sources to provide information when assessing credit risks. External sources are likely to be used more for new customers and internal sources for existing customers.

■ External sources include bank references, trade references, credit circles, credit rating agency reports, available accounts and other publications. Some organisations ask the customer to complete a credit application form which will provide the data it needs.

■ When using external sources of information the organisation will need to be aware of the restrictions of the Data Protection Act 1998 which regulates the disclosure of information about individuals (not companies) to third parties.

■ Internal sources of information include records of meetings, conversations and visits by a variety of employees of the organisation, including the sales ledger staff and sales force.

■ Another valuable exercise in credit assessment is the ratio analysis of financial accounts – preferably from three consecutive years. This will provide information about the trends in:
  • liquidity
  • profitability
  • the financial position

■ An organisation's credit control policy will often be formalised in a written Credit Policy document which ensures that all procedures are carried out correctly.

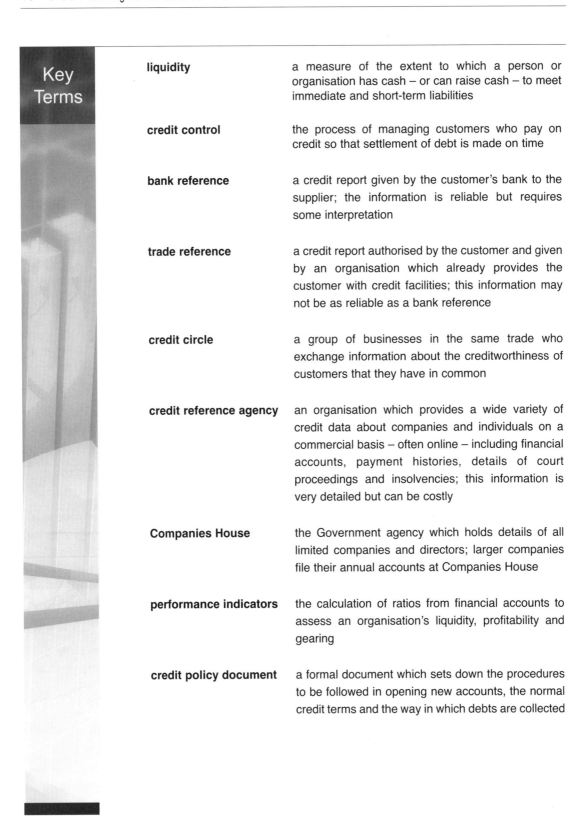

Key Terms

liquidity a measure of the extent to which a person or organisation has cash – or can raise cash – to meet immediate and short-term liabilities

credit control the process of managing customers who pay on credit so that settlement of debt is made on time

bank reference a credit report given by the customer's bank to the supplier; the information is reliable but requires some interpretation

trade reference a credit report authorised by the customer and given by an organisation which already provides the customer with credit facilities; this information may not be as reliable as a bank reference

credit circle a group of businesses in the same trade who exchange information about the creditworthiness of customers that they have in common

credit reference agency an organisation which provides a wide variety of credit data about companies and individuals on a commercial basis – often online – including financial accounts, payment histories, details of court proceedings and insolvencies; this information is very detailed but can be costly

Companies House the Government agency which holds details of all limited companies and directors; larger companies file their annual accounts at Companies House

performance indicators the calculation of ratios from financial accounts to assess an organisation's liquidity, profitability and gearing

credit policy document a formal document which sets down the procedures to be followed in opening new accounts, the normal credit terms and the way in which debts are collected

Activities

1.1 Liquidity management is important in a limited company business because:

(a) it ensures that shareholders should always receive a dividend

(b) it ensures that the company should be able to meet its short-term liabilities

(c) it ensures that the company should be able to meet its long-term liabilities

(d) it ensures that the company should always make a profit

Which one of these options is correct?

1.2 Credit control is a process which manages:

(a) the accounts of the receivables (debtors) of an organisation

(b) the accounts of the payables (creditors) of an organisation

(c) the bank accounts of an organisation

(d) the short-term investments of an organisation

Which one of these options is correct?

1.3 Possible sources of external information about a potential new customer include:

(a) bank references, trade references, other customers

(b) bank references, other customers, credit circles

(c) trade references, credit circles, credit rating agencies

(d) Companies House, credit rating agencies, HM Revenue & Customs

Which one of these options is correct?

1.4 A bank reference on a customer which states that the customer 'should prove good for your figures and purpose' means that:

(a) the customer is an excellent credit risk

(b) the customer is a very poor credit risk

(c) the customer's creditworthiness will eventually improve over time

(d) the customer's creditworthiness may need further investigation

Which one of these options is correct?

1.5 Information about a limited company customer received from a credit reference agency can include:

(a) financial accounts, payment history, directors' credit card numbers

(b) financial accounts, payment history, directors' names and addresses

(c) financial accounts, trade references, directors' names and addresses

(d) financial accounts, trade references, bank references

1.6 The Data Protection Act protects personal data held

(a) specifically relating to limited companies

(b) for a limited period of only three years

(c) specifically relating to individuals

(d) only in electronic records

1.7 Management accounts are useful in the assessment of a company's credit standing because they provide information about:

(a) liquidity, profitability, gearing

(b) liquidity, profitability, share value

(c) profitability, gearing, insurance cover

(d) profitability, insurance cover, share value

Which one of these options is correct?

1.8 Your company, GML Importers Limited, is processing a new credit application for S Low Limited. Steve Low, the customer's MD, is anxious that the facility be set up as soon as possible.

You find, however, that one of the trade references has not yet been received. You telephone the company concerned, but the manager who normally provides the references is away on holiday in Spain for the next two weeks.

Your colleague suggests using a credit reference agency to obtain a back-up reference. Describe:

(a) the data that a credit reference agency will be able to provide about a limited company

(b) one major advantage and one major disadvantage of using a credit reference agency

1.9 A sales ledger assistant at your company, GML Importers Limited, receives a telephone call from a competitor business, Pronto Importers, who ask if the person dealing with credit control can provide some information about your customer, Hal Johnson, who has approached them with a request to supply goods on credit terms.

They would like to know if you provide Hal Johnson with a credit limit, and if so, how much it is and whether your customer pays up on time. The sales ledger assistant is unsure how to deal with this request and asks you for advice. What would you advise? Give reasons for your recommendations.

1.10   You work for GML Importers Limited, an importer of toys from the Far East. The Credit Control Manager has received a letter from Toppo Toys Limited which operates a chain of 20 shops in the London area. Toppo Toys wishes to purchase stock from GML Importers Limited and is requesting credit facilities. You are to draft the text of a reply using today's date and your own name. The company Credit Policy Manual states that to assess any new proposition you will initially need a banker's reference and two trade references.

Toppo Toys Limited

71 Clerkenwell Avenue

London EC1R 5BC

Tel 0207 8371199 Fax 0207 8371192 Email sales@toppotoys.co.uk

D Brinkwell, Credit Control Manager
GML Importers Limited
29 The Greenway
Slough SL2 7GH

Dear Mr Brinkwell,

Request for credit facilities

We have purchased stock from you over the last six months and would now be grateful if you could consider providing us with credit facilities. We would initially be looking for a facility of £10,000 on thirty days terms.

As we have been trading with you on a cash terms basis for six months we hope that this can be arranged with the minimum of formality.

We look forward to hearing from you.

Yours sincerely

B Attman

Bart Attman
Director

---

2 Financial analysis of customer accounts

The last chapter mentioned the need for an organisation granting credit to obtain and analyse the financial accounts of:

* a prospective new business customer, or

* an existing business customer

It is possible that your assessment will involve a detailed analysis of this type and so a study of this chapter should be seen as useful preparation for your assessment.

This analysis involves the business obtaining the financial statements of the customer and carrying out the calculation of performance indicators.

The performance indicators normally required include:

* liquidity indicators

* profitability indicators

* debt indicators

* cash flow indicators

Your assessment may also require you to apply a credit scoring system to the performance indicators calculated.

This system will give a numerical value to the results of the performance indicators and the total of these values will then indicate the level of credit risk shown by the financial statements.

ANALYSING CUSTOMER ACCOUNTS

As we have seen in the last chapter, feedback from within the organisation is a valuable source of information for credit assessment. It is essential that it is backed up wherever possible by an analysis of past and up-to-date financial statements of the customer. If up-to-date financial statements are not available, draft accounts or internal management reports should be requested for analysis.

As you will appreciate this requirement will be more appropriate for the larger customers who prepare these types of accounts. Ideally, at least three years' accounts should be analysed in order to show the trends in three key areas:

- **liquidity** – the ability of the business to repay debts as they fall due
- **profitability** – the ability of the business to maintain its capital and to provide funds for repayment of debts in the future
- **gearing** – the financial risk taken on by the business shown by comparing interest bearing liabilities and total capital employed

You may well be familiar with the analysis of performance indicators from your other studies. If you are unsure about this subject, you are recommended to study Osborne Books' *Limited Company Accounts Tutorial*, Chapter 7, 'Interpretation of Financial Statements'.

what is a good indicator?

The question is often asked: what is a 'good' current ratio or a 'good' liquid capital ratio? The answer is that it is impossible to give a fail-safe answer. Businesses vary widely in the way their assets and liabilities are structured – compare a TV manufacturer and a supermarket, for example. There are some guidelines, however. These are shown below as notes, and should be used for guidance purposes only. We go on to look at **credit scoring** as a method of assessing credit risk in terms of performance indicators on page 28.

liquidity indicators

These indicators show the ability of the business to repay short-term debt from liquid or semi-liquid assets, and also to turn over its current assets such as inventory (stock) and receivables (debtors).

INDICATOR	FORMULA	WHAT IT SHOWS
current ratio	current assets / current liabilities	working capital expressed as a ratio *ideally 1.5 : 1 or higher*

liquid capital ratio	$\dfrac{\text{current assets} - \text{inventory}}{\text{current liabilities}}$	a ratio comparing liquidity with short-term debts, but excluding inventory *ideally 1 : 1 or higher*
inventory turnover (days)	$\dfrac{\text{inventory} \times 365}{\text{cost of sales}}$	the number of days on average that inventory is held *– this will depend entirely on the nature of the inventory; the figure should ideally not increase over time*
receivables turnover (days)	$\dfrac{\text{receivables} \times 365}{\text{sales}}$	the number of days on average that it takes for a receivable to pay up *– this will depend on the nature of the business; 30 to 60 days is common*
payables turnover (days)	$\dfrac{\text{payables} \times 365}{\text{purchases}}$	the number of days on average that it takes to pay a supplier *– this will usefully show how promptly the business pays its payables*

working capital cycle

Another useful indicator of liquidity is the **working capital cycle,** which uses the last three indicators relating to inventory, receivables and payables shown above:

- the average time that inventory is held ('inventory days')
- the average time that customers take to pay amounts due ('receivable days'), and
- the average time that is taken to pay suppliers the amounts that are owed ('payable days')

The working capital cycle can be calculated as follows:

**working capital cycle =
inventory days + receivable days – payable days**

The working capital cycle measures the period of time between payment for goods received into inventory and the collection of cash from customers in respect of the sale made to them.

The shorter the time between the initial outlay and the ultimate collection of cash, the lower the amount of working capital needed by the business.

profitability indicators

These indicators show the ability of the business to generate profit which will enable it to repay its debts in the longer term.

INDICATOR	FORMULA	WHAT IT SHOWS
profit from operations % **(operating profit)**	$\dfrac{\text{operating profit} \times 100}{\text{sales revenue}}$	profit made before deduction of tax and interest – *this should remain steady and in line with the industry average*
net profit %	$\dfrac{\text{net profit} \times 100}{\text{sales revenue}}$	profit made after deduction of all expenses – *this should ideally increase over the years, and not fall*
return on capital employed **(ROCE)**	$\dfrac{\text{profit from operations} \times 100}{\text{capital employed}^*}$ * total equity + non-current liabilities	profit made related to the capital employed by the company – *this should also remain steady over the years*

Interest cover measures the ability of a business to pay interest on borrowing from its profits:

interest cover	$\dfrac{\text{profit from operations}}{\text{interest}}$	the safety margin of profit over interest payable – *the higher the figure the better*

financial position

Financial position measures the strength and long-term financing of a company. The proportion of long-term debt to capital is known as **gearing**. This shows the extent to which the company is financed by debt. The first formula shown below includes current liabilities as well as long-term debt.

gearing %	$\dfrac{\text{total debt} \times 100}{\text{total debt} + \text{equity}}$	the relationship between total debt and capital – *this should ideally be less than 50%, the higher the figure, the less secure the company*

Another gearing formula, which excludes current liabilities, is as follows:

gearing %	$\dfrac{\text{long-term debt} \times 100}{\text{long-term debt} + \text{equity}}$	the relationship between long-term debt and capital

Another ratio sometimes used is the short-term debt ratio:

short-term debt ratio	$\dfrac{\text{short-term debt} \times 100}{\text{total debt}}$	the reliance on short-term debt by a business *– the lower the better because a reliance on short-term debt means the business may be less liquid*

cash flow indicators – EBITDA

EBITDA stands for:

Earnings **B**efore **I**nterest, **T**ax, **D**epreciation and **A**mortisation

This figure is calculated by deducting the **ITBA** entries in the income statement from the bottom-line net income. It gives an indication of the **cash earnings** of a business. (Note that 'amortisation' is the writing off of a liability, such as a loan, over a specified period of time).

There are two main extensions of the basic EBITDA indicator:

EBITDA interest cover	$\dfrac{\text{EBITDA}}{\text{interest payable*}}$ * from the income statement or statement of cash flows	the ability of a business to pay the interest on debt *– the higher the figure, the lower the risk*
EBITDA interest cover	$\dfrac{\text{EBITDA}}{\text{total debt}}$	a measure of the pay-back period of the debt *– the higher the figure, the higher the risk*

USING THE PERFORMANCE INDICATORS

So far in this chapter we have described and explained the performance indicators that you may be required to use in an assessment. The list is long, but you will be relieved to know that only a limited number will normally be required each time, as would be the case with most businesses carrying out a credit analysis. The point to remember is that the main areas of analysis are:

- **liquidity** – does the business have sufficient short-term resources to repay debt?
- **profitability** – does the business have the longer-term ability to generate cash to repay debt? (This can also involve EBITDA)
- **gearing** – how much debt is there already in relation to equity?

The Case Study which follows shows the credit assessment process in action and places performance indicators in the context of the other enquiries that need to be made when assessing a customer.

The chapter will then continue with a second Case Study explaining how credit scoring may be applied to the performance indicator results.

Case Study

FIRTH ELECTRONICS: CREDIT ASSESSMENT PROCEDURES

situation

You work in the credit control section of Firth Electronics. You have been approached by a new customer, Bridge Trading Limited for credit of £10,000 a month. You have sent out your normal enquiries – a bank credit status request and two trade credit reference requests. Bridge Trading have also sent you their last three years' accounts for you to analyse.

The replies and accounts summary are shown below.

You have been asked to prepare notes summarising your assessment of this company.

National Bank PLC

status report: Bridge Trading Limited

Request: £10,000 trade credit per month

Report: Good for your figure and purpose

Response to trade credit enquiry, received from A Jones & Co

Re: Bridge Trading Limited: £10,000 trade credit per month

We have been trading with this company for five years and allow £15,000 credit per month on 30 day terms. The company can sometimes take longer to pay than allowed by these terms.

Response to trade credit enquiry, received from A Patel

Bridge Trading Limited, £10,000 credit per month

We allow this customer £5,000 credit per month on 60 day terms. The account is usually paid on time, although sometimes payment can be late. The figure you quote is higher than the credit given by us but we know of no reasons why this customer should not be able to fulfil its liabilities.

SUMMARY OF FINANCIAL ACCOUNTS: BRIDGE TRADING LIMITED

	Year 1 £000	Year 2 £000	Year 3* £000
Sales revenue	1,000	1,200	1,400
Cost of sales	600	800	1,000
Current assets	880	1,040	1,200
Current liabilities	620	710	750
Inventory	200	220	280
Receivables	102	115	127
Payables	150	161	195
Profit from operations	80	94	112
Interest paid	20	34	32
Net profit	60	60	80
Long-term debt	200	200	250
Equity	400	460	520

*Year 3 was last year and the accounts were made up to 31 December.

solution

You process the data from the bank report, the two trade references and the three years' accounts, and set out the results in the table shown on the next page.

Note: you have been asked to calculate gearing on the total debt/total debt + equity basis.

ANALYSIS OF FINANCIAL ACCOUNTS: BRIDGE TRADING LIMITED

	Year 1	Year 2	Year 3
Current Ratio	1.42 : 1	1.46 : 1	1.60 : 1
Liquid Capital Ratio	1.10 : 1	1.15 : 1	1.23 : 1
Inventory turnover	122 days	100 days	102 days
Receivable days	37 days	35 days	33 days
Payable days	91 days	73 days	71 days
Net profit %	6%	5%	6%
Return on capital employed %	13.3%	14.2%	14.5%
Interest cover	4.0 times	2.8 times	3.5 times
Gearing	46.67%	43.97%	46.11%

You draw the following conclusions:

bank report

This indicates that the bank considers Bridge Trading Limited to be a reasonable credit risk, which, as far as bank reports go, is a positive response.

trade references

Both references draw attention to the fact that Bridge Trading Limited does pay up, but is often late in doing so. The analysis of the three years' accounts will therefore need to concentrate on the liquidity ratios. Late payment can either result from inefficiency or from poor liquidity.

analysis of three years' financial accounts

The profitability ratios (net profit and return on capital employed) and gearing percentage all suggest a company with manageable debt and a consistently sound profit record. The interest cover shows an ability to cover interest costs from profit.

The current ratio and liquid capital ratio have both improved over the three years, although the current ratio does reflect the high level of payables (see below). Receivable days at around 35 shows that the business is collecting its trade debts efficiently. It is the payment period (payable days) that gives cause for concern, although there has been some improvement. The reason is not a lack of liquidity, but is either a conscious policy of delaying payment to help with short-term financing, or just a lack of efficiency. Whatever, the reason, Firth Electronics should not accept similar treatment.

recommendation

Bridge Trading Limited should be allowed the credit requested, as there is sufficient liquidity in the company, but on strict 30 days' terms.

Payments should be carefully monitored and the company advised that any late payments could result in withdrawal of credit and an insistence on trading on cash terms only.

USING A CREDIT SCORING SYSTEM

Credit scoring is a system which give a numerical value to the results of the performance indicators calculated and the **total** of these values then indicates the **level of credit risk** shown by the financial statements. Normally a high score will indicate a low risk, and a low score a high risk. An example of a typical scoring system is shown below and explained on the next page.

CREDIT RATING (SCORING) SYSTEM	Score
Profit from operations margin	
Losses	–5
Less than 5%	0
5% and above but less than 10%	5
10% and above but less than 20%	10
20% and above	20
Interest cover	
No cover	–30
Less than 1	–20
More than 1 but less than 2	–10
More than 2 but less than 4	0
4 and above	10
Current ratio	
Less than 1	–20
Between 1 and 1.25	–10
Between 1.26 and 1.5	0
Above 1.5	10
Gearing (total debt/(total debt plus equity))	
Less than 25%	20
25% and above but less than 50%	10
More than 50% less than 65%	0
Between 65% and 75%	–20
Between 76% and 80%	–40
Above 80%	–100
Risk	**Aggregate score**
Very low risk	Between 60 and 21
Low risk	Between 20 and 1
Medium risk	Between 0 and –24
High risk	Between –25 and –50
Very high risk	Above –50

how to work out the score

It is possible that you will be asked in your assessment to process the performance indicators you have calculated to provide a credit score which will in turn indicate the level of credit risk shown by the accounts.

As you will see from the example shown on the previous page, the credit scoring system is set out in a table subdivided into sections for:

- the margin for the profit from operations (operating profit)
- interest cover
- current ratio
- gearing

In this way the credit scoring system covers all the main areas of concern: profitability, liquidity and gearing.

Let us assume we have already worked out the performance indicators results for two very contrasting businesses: Dodgee Ltd and Sound Ltd.

1 These are entered in the table below under the heading 'result'.

2 Using the table on the previous page we obtain a score (right-hand column) for each performance indicator required and apply it to the results in the table below and write it in the appropriate score column.

3 The score columns are totalled.

4 The scores are related to the 'aggregate score' section at the bottom of the credit score table on the opposite page and the level of risk identified.

5 The level of risk is entered on the bottom line of the table below. Sound Ltd has clearly done rather better than Dodgee Ltd.

Important note: this table has been set up in this text to illustrate the **method** of credit scoring you will need to adopt. If it is not provided in your assessment, you will find a format like this a useful way of organising your data.

	Dodgee Ltd		Sound Ltd	
performance indicator	*result*	*score*	*result*	*score*
Profit from operations margin	2%	0	10%	10
Interest cover	0.5	- 20	5	10
Current ratio	0.75 : 1	- 20	2.0 : 1.0	10
Gearing	70%	- 20	25%	10
Total score		- 60		40
Result		Very high risk		Very low risk

shortcomings of credit scoring

It should be pointed out that not all accounts will be credit scored in this way. In fact it is a rather arbitrary way of making a judgement of credit risk as it does not take in the other opinions that can be obtained from credit references given by banks, traders and other sources. For example it may be that you find out from the press that Sound Ltd (see the example on the previous page) is a major supplier to a manufacturer that has gone into liquidation. This could have a major effect on its future liquidity. Credit scoring would not tell you that.

There now follows a Case Study which covers the whole process of calculating performance indicators and credit scoring the results

Case Study

IPEX LIMITED: CREDIT ASSESSMENT AND CREDIT SCORING

situation

You work in the credit control section of Ipex Limited which uses a credit rating (scoring) system to assess the credit status of new and existing customers.

You have been asked to carry out three tasks on the last two years' accounts of Kennedy Enterprises Ltd, a new customer who has requested a £50,000 credit limit.

1   Calculate the performance indicators shown in the table below, using the financial data shown on the next page for both Year 2 and Year 1. You are to complete the 'Indicator' column below as appropriate.

2   Calculate the credit score on the basis of the table on page 32. You are to complete the 'Score' column below as appropriate.

3   State the level of risk shown by the credit score.

Kennedy Enterprises Limited	Indicator *Year 2*	Score *Year 2*	Indicator *Year 1*	Score *Year 1*
Operating profit margin %				
Interest cover				
Current ratio				
Gearing %				
Total score				

Accounts for Ipex Limited (extracts)	Year 2	Year 1
Income Statement	£'000	£'000
Sales revenue	18,000	16,000
Cost of sales	12,500	12,000
Gross profit	5,500	4,000
Distribution costs	1,700	1,700
Administration costs	1,200	1,200
Profit from operations	2,600	1,100
Interest payable	500	500
Profit on ordinary activities before taxation	2,100	600
Tax on profit on ordinary activities	700	200
Profit for the financial year	1,400	400
Statement of financial position	**Year 2**	**Year 1**
	£'000	£'000
Non-current assets		
Tangible assets	9,000	7,800
Current Assets		
Inventories	2,400	2,000
Trade Receivables	1,400	1,200
Cash	800	800
	4,600	4,000
Payables amounts falling due within one year		
Trade payables	3,000	2,600
Net current assets	1,600	1,400
Payables amounts falling due after more than one year		
Long term loans	5,000	5,000
Net assets	5,600	4,200
Equity		
Share capital	200	200
Retained earnings	5,400	4,000
Shareholders' funds	5,600	4,200

CREDIT RATING (SCORING) SYSTEM	Score
Profit from operations margin	
Losses	−5
Less than 5%	0
5% and above but less than 10%	5
10% and above but less than 20%	10
20% and above	20
Interest cover	
No cover	−30
Less than 1	−20
More than 1 but less than 2	−10
More than 2 but less than 4	0
4 and above	10
Current ratio	
Less than 1	−20
Between 1 and 1.25	−10
Between 1.26 and 1.5	0
Above 1.5	10
Gearing (total debt/(total debt plus equity))	
Less than 25%	20
25% and above but less than 50%	10
More than 50% less than 65%	0
Between 65% and 75%	−20
Between 76% and 80%	−40
Above 80%	−100
Risk	**Aggregate score**
Very low risk	Between 60 and 21
Low risk	Between 20 and 1
Medium risk	Between 0 and −24
High risk	Between −25 and −50
Very high risk	Above −50

solution

Tasks 1 and 2

See table below

Ipex Limited	Indicator *Year 2*	Score *Year 2*	Indicator *Year 1*	Score *Year 1*
Operating profit margin %	14.44%	10	6.88%	5
Interest cover	5.2	10	2.2	0
Current ratio	1.53 : 1	10	1.54 : 1	10
Gearing %	58.82%	0	64.41%	0
Total score		30		15

Task 3

The higher the total score, the lower the risk of the possible new customer, Kennedy Enterprises Ltd.

The Year 2 (ie the latest year) credit score is 30, which indicates a very low credit risk.

The Year 1 (ie previous year) credit score is 15, which indicates a low credit risk.

The credit risk has therefore improved over the two years, which is an excellent result. If all the other enquiries (eg bank and trade references) prove acceptable, Ipex Ltd should have no credit risk problems with Kennedy Enterprises Ltd and will be able to go ahead and offer appropriate credit terms, for example the requested £50,000 limit on 30 days terms.

Chapter Summary

- A valuable exercise in credit assessment is the ratio analysis of customer financial accounts – preferably from three consecutive years. Ratio analysis will extract performance indicators relating to:
  - liquidity
  - profitability
  - the financial position

  All of these will provide information about the customer's ability to repay invoices when they fall due.

  Individual performance indicators are listed in the Key Terms below.

- A technique used to assess the credit risk of an organisation is credit scoring. This applies a numerical value, known as a 'rating' or 'score' to a number of performance indicators and the total of these 'scores' is applied to a scale of risk which runs from very high risk (very low score) to very low risk (very high score).

- Credit scoring is a useful technique, but it must be used in combination with other assessment methods, for example bank and trade references, which may reveal information and trends not shown in purely numerical analysis.

Key Terms

liquidity indicators	performance indicators which show the extent of the liquidity of a business, ie its ability to repay short-term liabilities:	
current ratio	$\dfrac{\text{current assets}}{\text{current liabilities}}$	*working capital expressed as a ratio*
liquid capital ratio	$\dfrac{\text{current assets} - \text{inventory}}{\text{current liabilities}}$	*a ratio comparing liquidity with short-term debts, but excluding inventory*
inventory turnover (days)	$\dfrac{\text{inventory} \times 365}{\text{cost of sales}}$	*the number of days on average that inventory is held*
receivables turnover (days)	$\dfrac{\text{receivables} \times 365}{\text{sales}}$	*the number of days on average that it takes for a customer to pay up*
payables turnover (days)	$\dfrac{\text{payables} \times 365}{\text{purchases}}$	*the average number of days it takes to pay a supplier*
working capital cycle	inventory days + receivable days – payable days	*the time between payment for goods received and receipt of cash from customers*

profitability indicators   performance indicators which show the ability of the business to generate the profit needed to provide liquidity:

profit from operations %
(operating profit)

$$\frac{\text{operating profit} \times 100}{\text{sales revenue}}$$

profit made before deduction of tax and interest

net profit %

$$\frac{\text{net profit} \times 100}{\text{sales revenue}}$$

profit made after deduction of all expenses

return on capital employed
(ROCE)

$$\frac{\text{profit from operations} \times 100}{\text{capital employed}^*}$$

* total equity + non-current liabilities

profit made related to the capital employed by the company

interest cover

$$\frac{\text{profit from operations}}{\text{interest}}$$

the safety margin of profit over interest payable

---

financial position   the extent of the reliance of the business on external debt as opposed to capital – the less dependent the business is on external financing, the better it will be able to repay its own debts:

gearing % (total debt)

$$\frac{\text{total debt} \times 100}{\text{total debt} + \text{equity}}$$

the relationship between total debt and capital

gearing % (long-term debt)

$$\frac{\text{long-term debt} \times 100}{\text{long-term debt} + \text{equity}}$$

the relationship between long-term debt and capital

short-term debt ratio

$$\frac{\text{short-term debt} \times 100}{\text{total debt}}$$

the reliance on short-term debt by a business

EBITDA   **E**arnings **B**efore **I**nterest, **T**ax, **D**epreciation and **A**mortisation – gives an indication of the cash earnings of a business:

EBITDA interest cover

$$\frac{\text{EBITDA}}{\text{interest payable}^*}$$

* from the income statement or statement of cash flows

the ability of a business to pay the interest on debt

EBITDA interest cover

$$\frac{\text{EBITDA}}{\text{total debt}}$$

a measure of the pay-back period of the debt

Activities

2.1 You are assessing an application for a credit limit of £15,000 from a new customer, Stylo Limited. You have received a bank reference and two trade references. Stylo Limited has also provided you with a summary of its accounts for the last three years (see data below and on the next page).

Your company Credit Policy Manual requires that credit terms should initially be offered for a maximum of 30 days.

You are to:

(a) write comments on the bank reference

(b) write comments on the trade references

(c) analyse the accounts summary and draw up a table showing for the three years the following performance indicators:
- the current ratio and the liquid capital ratio
- receivable days and payable days
- net profit percentage
- interest cover and gearing (based on total debt and calculated to one decimal place)

(d) write comments on the performance indicators

(e) write a conclusion, stating your recommendations for the granting of the requested credit of £15,000

Centro Bank PLC

status report: Stylo Limited

Request: £15,000 trade credit per month

Report: Should prove good for your figure and purpose.

Response to trade credit enquiry, received from B Ruckner Ltd

Re: Stylo Limited: £15,000 trade credit per month

We have been trading with this company for five years and allow £10,000 credit per month on 60 day terms. The company normally meets its commitments on time.

Response to trade credit enquiry, received from V Williams

Stylo Limited: £15,000 credit per month

We allow this customer £5,000 credit per month on 60 day terms. The account is usually paid on time.

EXTRACT FROM FINANCIAL ACCOUNTS: STYLO LIMITED

	Year 1 £000	Year 2 £000	Year 3 £000
Sales revenue	750	781	720
Purchases	350	363	348
Current assets	720	705	684
Current liabilities	680	656	663
Inventory	200	220	280
Receivables	88	93	95
Payables	58	63	62
Profit from operations	80	86	94
Interest paid	60	71	80
Net profit	20	15	14
Long-term debt	121	150	190
Equity	125	145	145

2.2 You work for Ipex Limited in the credit control department and have been asked to credit score two new applications for credit:

1 De Gass Ltd is applying for a £30,000 credit limit

2 Vangov Ltd is applying for a £50,000 credit limit

You have been given the recent management accounts for both companies. These have been summarised and are set out in the schedules shown on pages 40 and 41.

You are to

(a) Calculate the performance indicators required by the tables set out on this page.

(b) Complete the tables with the required performance indicators.

(c) Credit score both schedules, using the credit scoring guidelines set out on the next page and completing the tables below with your results.

(d) State the level of credit risk of the two companies.

(e) State which of the two companies you would provide with credit terms.

(f) Explain the weaknesses exposed in the accounts of the company with the higher credit risk.

Customer: De Gass Limited	Indicator	Score
Operating profit margin %		
Interest cover		
Current ratio		
Gearing %		
Total score		

Customer: Vangov Limited	Indicator	Score
Operating profit margin %		
Interest cover		
Current ratio		
Gearing %		
Total score		

CREDIT RATING (SCORING) SYSTEM	Score
Profit from operations margin	
Losses	−5
Less than 5%	0
5% and above but less than 10%	5
10% and above but less than 20%	10
20% and above	20
Interest cover	
No cover	−30
Less than 1	−20
More than 1 but less than 2	−10
More than 2 but less than 4	0
4 and above	10
Current ratio	
Less than 1	−20
Between 1 and 1.25	−10
Between 1.26 and 1.5	0
Above 1.5	10
Gearing (total debt/(total debt plus equity))	
Less than 25%	20
25% and above but less than 50%	10
More than 50% less than 65%	0
Between 65% and 75%	−20
Between 76% and 80%	−40
Above 80%	−100
Risk	**Aggregate score**
Very low risk	Between 60 and 21
Low risk	Between 20 and 1
Medium risk	Between 0 and −24
High risk	Between −25 and −50
Very high risk	Above −50

Accounts for De Gass Limited (extracts)	
Income statement	*£'000*
Sales revenue	10,000
Cost of sales	7,000
Gross profit	3,000
Distribution costs	800
Administration costs	550
Profit from operations	1,650
Interest payable	210
Profit on ordinary activities before taxation	1,440
Tax on profit on ordinary activities	475
Profit for the financial year	965
Statement of financial position	
	£'000
Non-current assets	
Tangible assets	5,500
Current Assets	
Inventories	1,100
Trade Receivables	950
Cash	200
	2,250
Payables amounts falling due within one year	
Trade payables	1,500
Net current assets	750
Payables amounts falling due after more than one year	
Long term loans	1,500
Net assets	4,750
Equity	
Share capital	250
Retained earnings	4,500
Shareholders' funds	4,750

Accounts for Vangov Limited (extracts)	
Income statement	*£'000*
Sales revenue	12,000
Cost of sales	10,000
Gross profit	2,000
Distribution costs	750
Administration costs	680
Profit from operations	570
Interest payable	250
Profit on ordinary activities before taxation	320
Tax on profit on ordinary activities	105
Profit for the financial year	215
Statement of financial position	
	£'000
Non-current assets	
Tangible assets	4,000
Current Assets	
Inventories	2,000
Trade Receivables	550
Cash	50
	2,600
Payables amounts falling due within one year	
Trade payables	2,050
Net current assets	550
Payables amounts falling due after more than one year	
Long term loans	2,750
Net assets	1,800
Equity	
Share capital	100
Retained earnings	1,700
Shareholders' funds	1,800

3 Granting credit and setting up customer accounts

this chapter covers...

The last two chapters have described:

- *the credit assessment process which collects internal and external information about a customer who is asking for credit terms*

- *the analysis of management accounts by extracting performance indicators and using credit scoring techniques*

In this chapter we look in more detail at the next steps in the process:

- *making the decision whether or not to grant credit*

- *advising an unsuccessful applicant in a tactful way so that business is not lost*

- *setting up an account for a successful applicant requiring credit terms*

Setting up an account is a formal process establishing a legal relationship of contract between the supplier and the customer. This chapter describes:

- *general terms of supply and payment*

- *discounts – including settlement discounts*

- *payment of interest on late payment*

- *the use of credit insurance*

The credit control process is shown on the diagram on the next page. The dotted box denotes the stage that has been reached and is explained in this chapter.

The next chapter explains in detail the legal implications of a trading relationship.

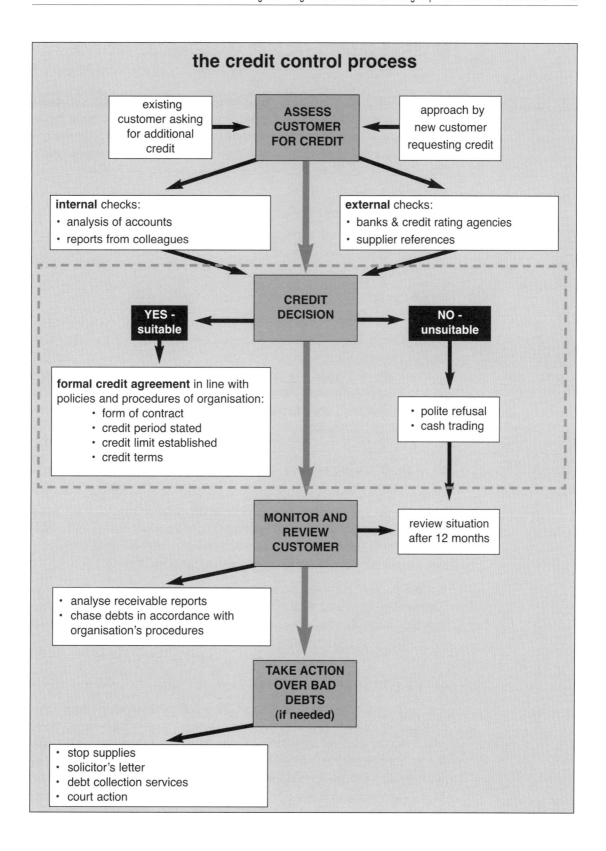

the credit control process

ASSESS CUSTOMER FOR CREDIT

existing customer asking for additional credit

approach by new customer requesting credit

internal checks:
• analysis of accounts
• reports from colleagues

external checks:
• banks & credit rating agencies
• supplier references

CREDIT DECISION

YES - suitable

NO - unsuitable

formal credit agreement in line with policies and procedures of organisation:
• form of contract
• credit period stated
• credit limit established
• credit terms

• polite refusal
• cash trading

MONITOR AND REVIEW CUSTOMER

review situation after 12 months

• analyse receivable reports
• chase debts in accordance with organisation's procedures

TAKE ACTION OVER BAD DEBTS (if needed)

• stop supplies
• solicitor's letter
• debt collection services
• court action

GRANTING CREDIT – FACTORS AFFECTING THE DECISION

The first chapter in this book concentrated on gathering sufficient information about a prospective customer so that a decision to grant credit can be made. It is important to appreciate that the decision will involve more than just the reading of references and the application of accounting ratios. Other factors to consider are

- ownership of the customer
- overseas customers
- amount of information available
- sales policy

ownership

Ownership of the customer will often determine the level of risk involved in granting credit. An organisation that has 'state' backing (eg the BBC or a local authority) will have a low risk status – ie it is very unlikely that the customer will fail to pay up on time. The same should be true of large companies and their subsidiary companies (which have their backing). It is the smaller organisations, eg start-up businesses, that are seen as being more risky, because failure rate in this sector is higher and bad debts more likely.

overseas companies

Overseas companies are a higher risk because of the possible problems the customer may have in obtaining and sending currency payments. Also, there will be complications with legal systems should it become necessary to take court action to recover debt. Consequently, trading with overseas customers may be on a 'cash up front' basis, at least to start with.

It must be stressed that overseas customers are not seen as being less creditworthy, it is just that the logistics of obtaining payment are more complex. Banks can be very helpful in this area in advising on country risk and setting up payment guarantee schemes.

insufficient information

It is possible that the amount of available information about a prospective customer is limited. This is particularly the case with a start-up business, which may be an excellently run company with good prospects, but the lack of any form of track record will make a credit decision hard to make. This situation may call for an initial refusal of credit with a promise of a review in, say, six months time when more information will have become available.

sales policy

There can be a tension within a commercial organisation between the sales function and the credit control function. Sales staff will want to obtain as many sales leads and new customers as possible in order to meet targets, even if the credit risks involved are higher than the credit control function would normally tolerate. The decision of whether or not to grant credit may therefore be swayed by current management policy, whether it be to 'play it safe' or to 'go all out for new sales'.

REFUSING CREDIT

The decision not to grant credit is a difficult one for all concerned. The organisation taking the decision is in danger of losing business because the potential customer may well go to another supplier; the potential customer will in turn lose both a supplier and a source of liquidity (remember that credit granted by a supplier = short-term financing).

The supplier is likely to suggest to the customer that cash trading (ie immediate 'on the nail' payment) would be an alternative until the credit status of the customer is reviewed in, say, six months time.

The supplier will have to treat the matter with great tact and diplomacy. A letter should be sent to the customer explaining the situation. The letter could incorporate some of the sentences shown below and should be written to relate to the circumstances of the case.

Dear Customer

Application for trade credit

'Thank you for your letter/application form of .... requesting credit of ....'

'We have assessed your application for credit using our usual criteria and have taken up references, but very much regret that we are unable to offer credit facilities to you at present.'

'We will be happy to review the situation again in six months time, when we have seen your latest financial accounts.'

'We very much value your custom and would be very pleased to trade with you on a cash basis for the time being. Our Sales Manager, Guy Weston, would be very interested in discussing this with you. His email address is gweston@gmlimporters.co.uk'

We look forward to hearing from you.'

---

half-way house credit

Some organisations, anxious not to lose a customer, might compromise and agree credit terms that are 'half-way' to what the customer requested. Examples of this are:

- shorter credit periods, eg 7 days rather than 30 days
- part payment, eg pay 25% cash terms and 75% after 30 days

This will not remove the risk of the customer not paying, but it reduces it, and may help to retain a good customer who would otherwise have gone to another supplier.

keeping to organisational policy

It must be stressed that all credit control decisions reached, whether a 'yes' or 'no' decision, must comply with the Credit Control Policy and Procedure Document used by the organisation, an example of which was given on page 14. Another example, taken from AAT Guidance material, is shown on the opposite page.

Note that the 'credit terms' section relates to the contents of this chapter.

CHANGES IN CREDIT TERMS

It may be that an existing customer will ask for a change in credit terms. This might be:

- a request for an increased limit, eg from £10,000 to £15,000
- a request for a longer payment period, eg an extension from 30 to 60 days

These may be requested with a certain amount of pressure from the customer – for example: "Ipex Limited, who also supply me, give me 60 days' credit, and we would not want to take our business away from you."

Whatever the circumstances, common sense and an analysis of the customer's trading history will be needed, together with a check on the Policies and Procedures requirements. In the case of a request to increase the limit, factors to examine will include:

- the amount of the increase – is it justified? – is it enough?
- has the customer kept within the existing limit?
- the trading history – have invoices been paid in full and on time?

If an extension of the credit period is required, the important thing is to check out the customer's liquidity. If the customer is experiencing cash flow problems one of the first solutions is to obtain longer credit from suppliers, effectively using the supplier to finance working capital shortages!

CREDIT CONTROL POLICIES AND PROCEDURES

New Accounts

1   One bank reference and two trade references are required.

2   A credit reference agency report and the last three years published accounts for limited companies need to be analysed.

3   A credit reference agency report and the last three years accounts for a sole trader need to be analysed.

Existing customers

4   A credit reference agency report to be obtained on an annual basis together with the latest annual accounts (either from Companies' House or directly from the customer). Both documents to be reviewed.

5   A trading history review to be undertaken annually to review for performance against credit limits and terms of payments.

6   Annual review of usage of the customers credit limit to ensure that an outdated credit limit is not in existence. This is particularly important where the trade with the customer has reduced over the past year.

Credit terms

7   Standard terms are 30 days from invoice. Any extension to be authorised by the Finance Director.

8   A 2% settlement discount to be offered to all accounts with a profit margin of 50% or greater, or with a profit margin of 30% and a value in excess of £50,000 or with the credit controllers discretion.

Debt collection process

9   Invoices to be despatched on day of issue, (day of issue to be no more than 2 days after date of delivery).

10   Statements to be despatched in the second week of the month.

11   Receivables analysis to be produced and reviewed on a weekly basis.

12   Reminder letter to be sent once an account is overdue.

13   Telephone chaser for accounts 15 days overdue.

14   Customer on stop list if no payment is received within 5 days of the telephone chaser. Computerised sales order processing system updated and automatic email sent to the customer contact and the account manager (sales person).

15   Letter threatening legal action if payment not received within 30 days of the first letter.

16   Legal proceedings / debt collection agency instructed subject to the approval of the Finance Director.

17   Prepare a report suggesting an appropriate provision for bad or doubtful debts.

18   If at any stage in the process the customer is declared insolvent or bankrupt then contact the insolvency practitioner in order to register the debt and notify the financial accountant so that the VAT can be reclaimed.

OPENING A NEW ACCOUNT

When the decision to grant credit has been taken, the account should be set up without delay and advised in writing to the customer, normally in a formal letter. This document will set out, in accordance with Policies and Procedures requirements:

- the period for which credit will be made available (eg 12 months)
- the limit on the account, eg £20,000
- the credit terms, eg 30 days from date of invoice
- discounts (including any settlement discount available)
- payment details (optional)
- interest penalties for late payment

This document is an important one for legal reasons. It can be referred to in later documentation, eg conditions of sale printed on the back of an order acknowledgement or invoice, and will be binding on the purchaser in the contract of sale which is set up each time a supply is made. We will explain in more detail about contracts of sale and legislation relating to selling in the next chapter. We will first explain the terms which will be set out in the letter to the customer when the account is opened.

credit period and limit

This limit is the upper limit which will be set on the sales ledger account of the new customer for a set period of time. A 'rule of thumb' calculation is that the limit should be twice the average monthly sales expected to be made to the customer. The period of the limit is normally twelve months.

credit terms

A number of credit payment terms need explanation. Note the distinction between 'net' – which refers to the timing of the supply of goods or services – and the use of the invoice date to calculate the payment date.

cash terms	immediate payment, ie zero credit
30 days from date of invoice	payment is due 30 days after the invoice date, eg payment of an invoice dated 10 March is due by 10 April
net monthly	payment of one month's supplies of goods or services is due at the end of the following month, eg payment of a delivery dated 10 March is due by 30 April

net 30 days payment of a supply of goods/services is due 30 days after the delivery (the same principle is applicable to 'net 60 days' etc)

discounts

A discount is a percentage reduction in the selling price.

Trade discount is traditionally given to established customers who buy on a regular basis, although a new customer may be given it straightaway, particularly if it has been requested as part of a 'deal' to open the account. The amount will vary according to the product. For example, a textbook like this one may sell to a bookshop at a trade discount of around 30%.

Settlement discount (also known as cash discount) is a percentage reduction in selling price allowed when settlement is made earlier than normal, eg '2.5% discount for settlement within 7 days'. For example, a purchaser receiving an invoice for £100 (ignoring VAT) with these terms will only have to pay £97.50 (ie £100 less £2.50 discount).

Settlement discount is attractive **when interest rates are high**. This is because money that may otherwise have been borrowed on overdraft by the seller to finance working capital – at a high interest rate – will be paid into the bank earlier and the interest cost will be reduced accordingly.

Alternatively, **when interest rates are high**, the seller could invest the cash received earlier through settlement discount at an attractive interest rate.

If interest rates are low, the cost to the seller of offering settlement discount (ie the reduction in the selling price) can be comparatively high, which makes it less attractive. The **annual equivalent** of the cost can be worked out by the formula shown below. The cost is worked out on an annual equivalent basis so that it can be compared with interest rates (also quoted per annum):

$$\left[\frac{d}{100-d}\right] \times \left[\frac{365}{N-D}\right] \times \quad 100\% \quad = \quad \text{annual cost of discount}$$

Where d   =   settlement discount percentage

N   =   normal settlement period in days

D   =   settlement period for early payment in days

Another disadvantage of offering settlement discount is that customers will take it and then pay the reduced amount later than the specified date! There is very little that can be done about this practice. With all these factors in mind, it is no surprise that settlement discounts are comparatively rare.

worked example – the cost of offering settlement discount

Your business is considering offering 1.5% settlement discount for payment of invoices within seven days rather than the thirty days normally offered. How much is it going to cost your business on an annual basis? How does it compare with the 8% it might cost you to finance the invoice on a bank overdraft? How does it compare with investment rates available at the time?

solution

The formula is

$$\left[\frac{d}{100-d}\right] \times \left[\frac{365}{N-D}\right] \times 100\% = \text{annual cost of discount}$$

d	= settlement discount percentage	=	1.5%
N	= normal settlement period in days	=	30
D	= settlement period for early payment	=	7

The calculation is

$$\left[\frac{1.5}{98.5}\right] \times \left[\frac{365}{23}\right] \times 100\% = \text{annual cost of discount} = 24.17\%$$

This shows that the annual cost to the business will be 24.17% which is more expensive than financing the extra 23 days (ie 30 less 7 days) on overdraft at 8% per annum. Cash discount therefore does not look like a good idea.

Also, if the business was considering investing the cash received 23 days earlier, the investment rate would need to be in excess of 24.17% to make it at all worthwhile; this is extremely unlikely.

payment details

Payment can be made in a number of different ways, and these can have a cost implication. Generally speaking, payment by cheque and cash is more expensive both for the customer and the supplier in terms of handling costs and bank charges.

Many organisations actively encourage computer payments through the BACS system which transfers money from one account to another by computer. When setting up an account, the seller may request BACS payments instead of cheque payment.

interest penalties for late payment

It is common practice for organisations to include in their terms and conditions the right to charge interest on late payments. Not many organisations will necessarily enforce this right, because they then run the risk of alienating and losing the customer. The terms are normally included as an incentive to pay.

The first extract below is taken from the terms and conditions on account opening documentation. The second extract is taken from the terms printed on the back of an acknowledgment of an order.

Our terms are strictly 30 days net monthly. Interest will be charged at 2% per month (or part thereof) on all amounts unpaid after the due date.

If payment is not made when due the Company may cancel this contract and any other contract between the Customer and the Company, suspend any further deliveries and/or charge interest accruing on a daily basis on any amount unpaid by the Customer at a rate of 2 per cent per calendar month or part thereof that payment remains outstanding.

Interest on late payment is also enforceable in law, although, as mentioned above, organisations are only likely to take this action as a last resort. The statute is the **Late Payment of Commercial Debts (Interest) Act 1998** and the interest rate that can be charged is the Bank of England official dealing (base) rate plus 8%. It should be noted that there does not need to be a mention of this law in the 'terms and conditions' issued by the seller – it is an automatic legal right.

retention of title (ROT)

Another term which sometimes appears on the front of invoices and in the small print on the back of sales documents is that ownership of the goods sold does not pass to the buyer until payment has been made. This is known as a **retention of title** clause or by its quaint acronym 'ROT.'

This may sound an odd arrangement, but it is included so that in the unlikely event of the buyer becoming bankrupt/insolvent, the seller may attempt to reclaim the goods and so get some money back. This is workable when the goods are easily identifiable, such as books or packets of crisps, but causes problems when the goods are raw materials, eg blank paper or potatoes.

An example of a retention of title clause is shown below.

5. Title in all Goods supplied by the Company shall vest in the Company until the Company has received full payment in respect thereof.

CREDIT INSURANCE

UK sales – credit insurance

Credit insurance replaces cash lost when a debt goes bad. Specialised companies such as Eulen Hermes and Coface UK offer tailor-made solutions for different types and sizes of organisation. Typical options include:

- **whole turnover insurance** – general (up to 90%) coverage in the case of debtor default (non-payment of debts)
- insurance limited to **key accounts** – up to 40 customers with up to 100% coverage
- **single account** insurance – 100% cover

Premiums will depend on the risk involved and the insurer will insist on credit analysis of larger customers.

Credit insurance – if it is taken – is therefore an integral part of the credit control process. Businesses may decide to insist on credit insurance for doubtful risk customers in times of recession, but they do face the danger that the insurance may be withdrawn if a particular business becomes uninsurable. The retail store Woolworths suffered this fate, as was reported in the Press at the time:

> *'Shares in Woolworths have been hit by the credit insurance refusal, falling by over 16% amid fears that suppliers to the chain are likely to insist on payment before shipping goods rather than trade on credit terms.'*

As suggested here, if a business is faced with a request for credit from a company from which credit insurance has been withdrawn, the company must be told tactfully that trading can only proceed on a 'cash' basis.

overseas sales – export credit insurance

Businesses that sell goods and services abroad are often advised to set up **export credit insurance**. This covers:

- the **credit risk** of selling to an overseas buyer – inevitably it is more difficult to chase up overseas debts, and should the debt turn bad, it is likely to prove difficult to bring court action against the customer
- the **political risk** of selling to a country where the political situation is less stable and might produce a revolution, civil war or economic collapse, all of which would reduce the possibility of receiving payment

Export credit insurance cover is available from **private sector commercial companies** for the supply of consumer goods and services sold on credit.

Chapter
Summary

■ The decision to grant credit involves a variety of different factors involving levels of risk: internal and external credit information, the nature of the ownership of the organisation, its location (UK or overseas), the amount of information available and the level of risk attached to the sales policy.

■ If credit is to be refused, the communication of the refusal to the potential customer should be carried out in a tactful and diplomatic way, and the opportunity to trade on a cash basis offered.

■ Some organisations may be willing to compromise and offer limited credit terms to a partially risky customer; these terms might include a shorter credit period or acceptance of part payment of invoices.

■ Customers may ask for a change in credit terms, for example an increase in limit or an extension in the payment period. The proposition should be viewed in the light of the amount involved and the customer's trading history.

■ When the decision to grant credit has been made, the supplier should set out the credit terms in writing for the customer. This should include:
    - the credit period
    - the credit limit
    - the payment terms
    - details of discounts
    - payment instructions
    - interest penalties on late payment

■ The granting of settlement discount is normally more cost effective when interest rates are high. The annual cost of granting the discount can be calculated by formula and compared with the current cost of borrowing, or interest rates for investing the money.

■ Penalties on late payment can be written into the credit terms as required. There is also a statutory right to claim interest on late payments under the Late Payment of Commercial Debts (Interest) Act 1998. Sellers of goods often include a 'Retention of Title (ROT) clause in their documentation.

■ Credit insurance can be useful cover for avoiding bad debts and may be required as part of the credit control policy. It has the weakness, however, that it may be withdrawn from businesses which are experiencing severe cash-flow problems

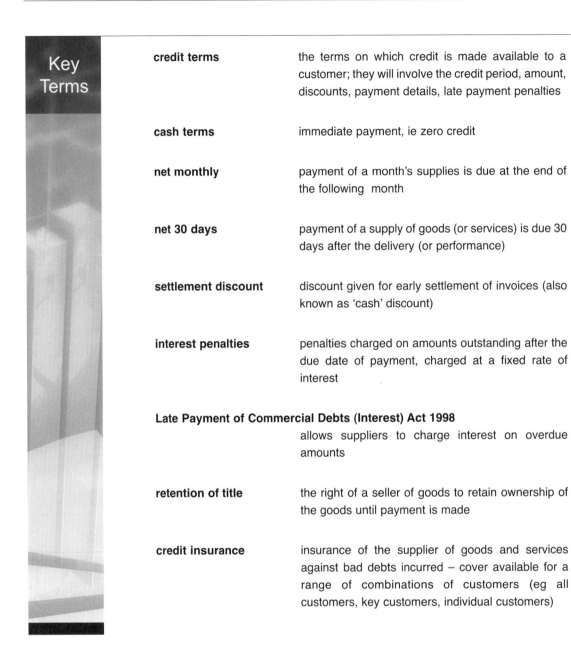

Key Terms

credit terms
the terms on which credit is made available to a customer; they will involve the credit period, amount, discounts, payment details, late payment penalties

cash terms
immediate payment, ie zero credit

net monthly
payment of a month's supplies is due at the end of the following month

net 30 days
payment of a supply of goods (or services) is due 30 days after the delivery (or performance)

settlement discount
discount given for early settlement of invoices (also known as 'cash' discount)

interest penalties
penalties charged on amounts outstanding after the due date of payment, charged at a fixed rate of interest

Late Payment of Commercial Debts (Interest) Act 1998
allows suppliers to charge interest on overdue amounts

retention of title
the right of a seller of goods to retain ownership of the goods until payment is made

credit insurance
insurance of the supplier of goods and services against bad debts incurred – cover available for a range of combinations of customers (eg all customers, key customers, individual customers)

Activities

3.1 A 'rule of thumb' calculation for the size of a credit limit granted to a customer is based on an amount equal to:

(a) 50% of the estimated annual sales turnover of the customer's account

(b) 50% of the amount of the turnover of the customer's account covered by credit insurance

(c) one month's turnover of the customer's account

(d) two month's turnover of the customer's account

Which one of these options is correct?

3.2 'Net monthly' terms on a credit account means that:

(a) payment must be made within one month of the actual invoice date

(b) payment of one month's invoices is due at the end of the following month

(c) each month's payment is made net of deduction of settlement discount

(d) the settlement is made online via the internet

Which one of these options is correct?

3.3 A business is most likely to gain an advantage from offering settlement discount for early payment of invoices when:

(a) overdraft interest rates are high

(b) overdraft interest rates are low

(c) the trade discount rate is low

(d) the trade discount rate is high

Which one of these options is correct?

3.4 ABC Ltd's terms of payment are 28 days. It is offering a discount of 1% for payment within 7 days. Bella Donna owes £100. The amount the customer will pay if she takes advantage of the discount, and the simple annual interest rate will be:

(a) £97.50 and 44.57%

(b) £99.00 and 17.38%

(c) £99.00 and 17.56%

(d) £98.50 and 26.47%

Which one of these options is correct?

3.5   Credit insurance allows a company to claim for amounts owed:

(a)   by the company to the bank when company liquidity is low

(b)   by the company's customers when their debts become bad debts

(c)   by company employees who have used company credit cards and have left the company

(d)   by the company to suppliers when a retention of title clause is operating

Which one of these options is correct?

3.6   The Late Payment of Commercial Debts (Interest) Act allows:

(a)   suppliers to charge interest on overdue amounts owing

(b)   banks to increase interest charged on loans when repayments are delayed

(c)   customers to delay payment of invoices when their liquidity is low

(d)   customers to delay payment of invoices when settlement discount is offered

Which one of these options is correct?

3.7   A retention of title (ROT) clause states that:

(a)   customers retain title to the goods supplied as long as they can be identified

(b)   customers retain title to the goods supplied until they are paid for

(c)   suppliers retain title to the goods supplied until they are paid for and can be identified

(d)   suppliers retain title to the goods supplied when they cannot be identified

3.8   An invoice for goods supplied is dated 27 April. The goods are delivered on 2 May.

When is the invoice due for payment if the terms are:

(a)   30 days of date of invoice?

(b)   net monthly?

(c)   net 30 days?

3.9   (a)   What is the annual cost to an organisation of granting settlement discount of 1.5% for settlement within 30 days? The normal payment period granted is 60 days.

(b)   Would granting settlement discount be an attractive option for the seller if the cost of borrowing on overdraft was

(i)   15% p.a.

(ii)   25% p.a.

Give reasons for your answers.

3.10 You work in the credit control section of RPG Limited. The company has recently received an application for £45,000 credit terms from a new customer, Artax Limited.

The normal bank and trade credit enquiries have been made and have produced a positive result.

Artax have provided two years' accounts which have been analysed and credit scored. The results of this analysis and the credit scoring ratings are shown below.

Artax Limited	**Indicator** Year 2	**Score** Year 2	**Indicator** Year 1	**Score** Year 1
Profit from operations margin %	6.97%	0	25.14%	10
Interest cover	2.2	- 10	4.1	10
Current ratio	1.10 : 1	0	2.1 : 1	5
Gearing %	65.22%	- 10	46.17%	10
Total score				

The internal policy documentation of RPG Limited provide the following guidelines for granting of credit based on the credit score obtained.

CREDIT SCORING RISK CRITERIA		
Total score	**Risk level**	**Action**
60 to 21	Very low	Accept
20 to 1	Low	Accept
0 to - 24	Medium	Refer to Financial Director (cash trading recommended)
- 25 to - 49	High	Unacceptable
- 50 and lower	Very high	Unacceptable

You are to:

(a) Work out the total credit score for the last two years by completing the table above.

(b) State the credit risk for Year 1 and Year 2.

(c) Recommend a course of action.

(d) Prepare the text of a suitable reply to Artax Limited.

3.11 You work in the credit control section of RPG Limited. The company has recently received an application from an existing customer, Hermes Limited, for an increase in their credit limit.

The current limit is £50,000 and they wish to increase this to £90,000 following a recent period of expansion in trading by the company.

The most recent credit scoring of the accounts of Hermes Limited produced the following results:

Hermes Limited	Indicator Year 2	Score Year 2	Indicator Year 1	Score Year 1
Profit from operations margin %	15.32%	0	22.34%	10
Interest cover	2.1	– 10	4.1	0
Current ratio	1.03 : 1	0	1.5 : 1	5
Gearing %	65.22%	– 10	51.17%	0
Total score		– 20		15

The credit score totals indicate that the credit risk level over the two years increased as follows:

Year 1:   15 credit score   = Low risk

Year 2:   – 20 credit score   = Medium risk

According to the Credit Control Policies and Procedures of the company, this greater level of risk means that the request for an increase in credit limit will need to be referred to the Financial Director for approval.

In order to prepare for this proposal to go to the Finance Director, you decide to:

- research your records for details of Hermes Limited's trading history

- contact Hermes Limited for more up-to-date financial data – you have noticed that the credit-scored data shown above is nearly nine months out of date

The results of your findings are as follows:

trading history

Hermes Limited, after some excesses last year, has consistently traded within the £50,000 credit limit for the last six months.

Hermes Limited always settles its account within the stipulated 30 days period.

recent financial data

The following figures were taken from the six-monthly management accounts produced by Hermes Limited (see the table on the next page):

	£000s
Sales revenue	2,000
Profit from operations	640
Interest payable	80
Current assets	2,600
Current liabilities	1,300
Total debt	1,750
Equity	2,000

Tasks

(a) Using the latest financial figures in the table above, calculate the four key performance indicators listed on the table on the previous page. You do not have to carry out any credit scoring.

Draw up a table comparing these four performance indicators with those from Year 2.

(b) Write brief comments on the trend shown by each of the performance indicators, stating how they will reflect on the credit rating of Hermes Limited. Include a brief general conclusion stating whether or not you consider the credit limit should be increased.

(c) Write the text of an email to your Finance Director giving your recommendation, with reasons, for the acceptance or refusal of the request for the increase in limit from £50,000 to £90,000.

4 Running customer accounts – legal considerations

this chapter covers...

The last chapter described the practicalities of:

- *setting up a credit account for a customer*

- *assessing credit risk*

- *dealing with requests for an increase in a credit limit*

- *refusing credit*

You also have to know about the legal framework which governs a trading relationship. This can involve:

- *the law of contract, which has been established over the centuries between sellers and buyers and is part of common law – ie it is not set down in Acts of Parliament*

- *legislation, which is law covering specific areas such as the sale of goods and services, and is set down in Acts of Parliament*

Specific legislation covered in this chapter includes:

- *Trade Descriptions Act*

- *Sale of Goods Act*

- *Consumer Credit Act*

- *Unfair Contract Terms Act.*

The next chapter describes how an account is monitored, with the overall aim of reducing the incidence of bad debts.

CUSTOMERS AND CONTRACTS

Part of your course involves the understanding of the legal framework which enables buying and selling to take place and which states what can happen if there is a dispute. The agreement between the parties is known as a **contract**.

what is a contract?

a contract is a legally binding agreement enforceable in a court of law

Contracts, which may be in writing, or by word of mouth (oral), are agreements between two parties. Examples include:

- a written contract which you sign if you issue a purchase order for goods

- an oral contract if you have a meeting with a supplier and agree to buy a certain quantity of specified goods

- an oral contract if you order goods over the telephone

In each case somebody does something for which some kind of payment is made. A contract is **an agreement with legal consequences** because if the work done is not satisfactory, or if the payment is not made, the wronged party can take the other person to court for **breach of contract.**

Contract law affects many business arrangements, including the granting of credit. For example if you quote an incorrect price to a customer, they may be able to hold your business to that price, under the terms of the contract of sale. If you fail to finish a job for a customer, they may be able to go to court to obtain a court order for your business to complete the work under the contract.

the three elements of a contract

There are three elements which are common and essential to all contracts:

elements of a contract

agreement – an offer and an acceptance

bargain – some value (consideration) passes

intention to create legal relations – the agreement is commercial

THE AGREEMENT – OFFER AND ACCEPTANCE

the offer

An **offer** may be made by:

- the **seller** of goods and services to an individual, a group, or generally to anyone who wishes to make a purchase, or . . .

- the **buyer** of goods and services who wishes to place a definite order for goods or services using a signed purchase order or an online authorisation for an online purchase

The acceptance of an offer – from the seller or the buyer – will then form the basis of a **legally binding contract** which can be upheld in a court of law. At the time the contract is formed various terms and conditions relating to price, quantity and discount can be agreed and form an integral part of the agreement (see pages 66-67 for an example).

invitation to treat

An offer is quite different from an **invitation to treat** which is an invitation to a person to make an offer. Goods on supermarket shelves, for example, are an invitation for a customer to put them in a trolley and go to the checkout where the customer can offer to purchase the goods at the price indicated **at the checkout**, which is where the **contract** takes place.

A business offering its goods for sale in a catalogue (paper-based or online) is also making an invitation to treat. The customer seeing the catalogue can then proceed to issue a purchase order or place the order online at the current price which will be agreed between the supplier and the customer.

---

practical example – invitation to treat

problem
Basil sees a computer advertised in the local paper for £50. He telephones the computer supplier who tells him that the figure is a printing error – it should have been £500. Basil is angry and insists on buying his computer for £50. The problem is, does a contract exist on the basis of the £50 quoted?

answer
Basil has no rights here. There is no contract because the £50 quoted is only **an invitation to treat**, an invitation for Basil to buy the computer. The company will clearly not agree to £50 for a new computer.

termination of an offer

An offer may only be accepted while it is still open for acceptance. An offer may be terminated in the following circumstances:

- the time limit (if there is one) expires; if there is no time limit the offer lapses after a reasonable period of time
- the offeror – the person making the offer – may revoke (cancel) the offer
- an offer may be rejected by the making of a counter-offer; for instance, if you offer your car for sale for £1,500 and someone offers you £1,350, that is a counter-offer
- by acceptance or rejection of the offer

acceptance of an offer

Acceptance of an offer must be firm and unambiguous; it may be in spoken words, written form or even implied by action. Acceptance cannot be assumed from silence on the part of the person to whom the offer is made. For instance, if you say "I offer you my car for £1,500; if I have not heard from you within a week I will assume the deal is done", there is no acceptance. The offeree may go on holiday, or forget it even happened.

Acceptance must also be **unconditional**. Any new term introduced – "I will agree to buy your car as long as the wing is resprayed" – amounts to a counter-offer and will revoke the original offer.

The term "**subject to contract**", often seen on estate agents' boards, means that the terms of the offer to the offeree are agreeable, but have not been finally accepted. The two parties involved have agreed to draw up a formal contract for signature at a later date. There is no binding contract at this point.

The rules relating to **communication of acceptance** are largely dictated by what is required by the offer:

- the acceptance must normally be communicated to the person making the offer
- if the offer requires acceptance by a specific means (letter/fax/verbal message/email) then that means must be used for the acceptance to be effective

THE BARGAIN: CONSIDERATION

A valid contract involves a bargain, a passing of value, known in law as **consideration**. If a business buys goods there is a two way process involved:

- the supplier promises to deliver the goods
- the buyer agrees to pay for them

The parties involved are the promisor, the supplier that promises to supply the goods and the promisee, the buyer who has to make payment. The **consideration** here is the 'value' given by both parties:

- the payment – the price paid by the buyer for the goods provided
- the value of the goods handed over by the seller

There are a number of legal rules which relate to consideration:

consideration must be sufficient

Consideration must by law be sufficient. This means that:

- it must have value, although the value need not be adequate in some eyes; for example, you could sell this book for 5p; many might think the amount to be inadequate, but the 5p still has value and is therefore consideration
- it must be sufficient, ie it must be in return for the promise; money due for some other reason or obligation is not sufficient consideration

consideration – other issues

The person who is promised goods or a service **must themselves provide payment** if the promise is to be enforceable as a contract. If you buy goods, you must make the payment. If someone else pays for you (an unlikely event!) you cannot take the supplier to court if the goods do not arrive.

Also, the consideration **should not happen before the promise**. If you mend someone's car without any mention of payment, and the car owner the following week promises to give you £50, and subsequently refuses to pay you, there is no contract. The promise of payment followed the service provided.

---

practical example – consideration

problem
Basil runs a computer maintenance business and promises to repair a computer for a friend free of charge one weekend. Unfortunately Basil wipes all the data from the computer and it cannot be replaced. His friend says he will sue Basil. Can he? Is there a contract?

answer
No. There is no contract because there is no consideration – no money has been paid. Basil has made a mistake but he cannot be sued.

THE INTENTION TO CREATE LEGAL RELATIONS

A contract is an agreement involving consideration which the parties intend to be legally binding. In other words the parties entering a contract can reasonably expect the agreement to be enforced in a court of law if the need arises. The law assumes:

- commercial agreements are intended to be legally binding
- social and domestic arrangements are not intended to be legally binding

In short, if a person enters a contract to buy your car and then, without reason, refuses to pay for it, you can take him or her to court. If you ask a friend out for the evening, promising to take him or her out for a meal, and your friend doesn't turn up, you can not take court action. The sale of a car involves the intention to create legal relations, the invitation out does not.

BREACH OF CONTRACT

A contract normally contains certain terms which must be fulfilled as part of the agreement. If a person breaks one of those terms, that person is in **breach of contract**. For example, if a supplier undertakes to supply goods, it must send the goods on the due date, and in turn expects the goods to be paid for by a certain time. If the customer does not pay, he or she is in breach of contract and may be taken to court for **damages** (money compensation).

Contract terms may be classified as follows:

express terms   explicitly stated terms which are binding on both parties to the contract

conditions   fundamental terms of the contract which, if broken, will enable the injured party to reject the contract and to go to court to sue for damages

warranties   minor terms which if broken can be cause for an action for damages for loss suffered; the contract, however, remains in force

implied terms   terms which are not stated, but which are implied by trade custom or by law; for instance, goods sold should be of "satisfactory quality", in accordance with the Sale of Goods Act

In short:

- express terms are written into the contract; implied terms are not
- conditions are important terms, warranties are less important

remedies for breach of contract

Legal action can be taken against a customer when a contract is in existence because non-payment is a **breach of contract** – the receivable (debtor) is not carrying out an agreed part of the contract.

There are a number of **remedies** available for breach of contract in a wide variety of situations. A common legal term used is **damages**, which is **money compensation for loss or injury.**

The actual remedy chosen will depend on the type of contract. For example, a builder who is contracted to build a house and disappears off site before putting the roof on, can be ordered by the court to complete the work – this is the remedy of **specific performance**.

If, however, the person having the house built refuses the builder access to the site for some reason or other, the builder could terminate the contract and demand payment for what had been done – this is the remedy of **quantum meruit**, which means 'what it deserves'. In other words, the law assumes a promise made by the employer to the builder that he will pay him for his work, as much as he may deserve or merit.

These situations do not have much in common with credit control in an organisation. Here the remedy of **action for the price** – ie taking legal action in the courts for recovery of an unpaid debt – is the normal remedy for breach of contract involving a receivable.

TERMS OF COMMERCIAL CONTRACTS

It is normal business practice for the seller to make sure that when goods or services are sold that the **terms and conditions of sale** – ie the price and payment terms – are clearly set out in the contract granting credit. If there is then any problem, late payment or non-payment for example, the supplier can hold the customer to the stated terms, in a court of law if necessary.

These terms are often printed on the back of the order acknowledgement or invoice issued by the supplier, as in the example extract shown on the next page. The terms here include:

1 the supplier's terms take precedence over the customer's terms

2 the supplier is not bound by prices in the catalogue (this is a reinforcement of the fact that these prices are an invitation to treat)

3 the supplier can ask for references and also cancel a credit limit if needed

4 payment is to be made on 30 days on invoice terms

5 retention of title clause (see page 51)

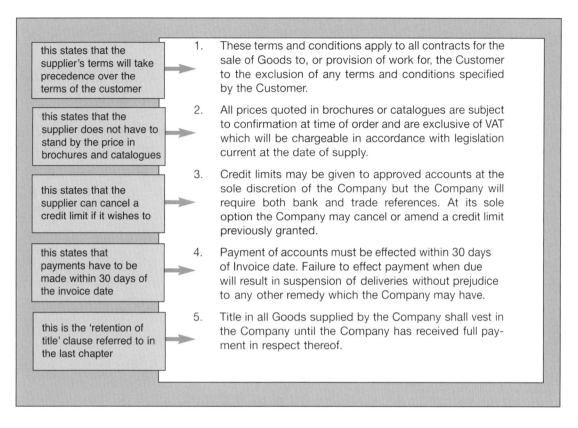

The following annotations appear to the left of the numbered clauses:

this states that the supplier's terms will take precedence over the terms of the customer →

1. These terms and conditions apply to all contracts for the sale of Goods to, or provision of work for, the Customer to the exclusion of any terms and conditions specified by the Customer.

this states that the supplier does not have to stand by the price in brochures and catalogues →

2. All prices quoted in brochures or catalogues are subject to confirmation at time of order and are exclusive of VAT which will be chargeable in accordance with legislation current at the date of supply.

this states that the supplier can cancel a credit limit if it wishes to →

3. Credit limits may be given to approved accounts at the sole discretion of the Company but the Company will require both bank and trade references. At its sole option the Company may cancel or amend a credit limit previously granted.

this states that payments have to be made within 30 days of the invoice date →

4. Payment of accounts must be effected within 30 days of Invoice date. Failure to effect payment when due will result in suspension of deliveries without prejudice to any other remedy which the Company may have.

this is the 'retention of title' clause referred to in the last chapter →

5. Title in all Goods supplied by the Company shall vest in the Company until the Company has received full payment in respect thereof.

more terminology relating to contracts

There are some further terms relating to contracts which you should be aware of. When you read through these terms you will see that most of them are not likely to affect commercial contracts for the granting of credit – or at least you will hope that this will not be the case!

- **capacity** – a person (and this includes a limited company) must have the legal capacity to enter into a contract; people who do not have capacity include, for example, minors (people under 18), people of unsound mind, alien enemies and drunkards

- **consent** – a contract and any amendment to a contract requires the consent of all parties to the contract

- **void contracts** – a contract which is basically against the principles of the law, for example a contract killing

- **voidable contracts** – contracts which may be set aside because one of the parties entered into it when pressurised to do so, or when he or she was drunk or insane.

- **unenforceable contracts** – a contract that is valid (ie it is not void), but the court will not enforce it – a contract of prostitution (which is legal in English law), for example

SELLING AND STATUTE LAW

There are a number of statutes (Acts of Parliament) which govern the way in which goods and services are sold, and these obviously affect the way in which businesses operate.

Note that a credit control department cannot exclude these statutes through clever wording of terms and conditions. They are part of English statute law and are binding on all relevant business dealings.

The principal statutes are the Trade Descriptions Act, the Sale of Goods Act (as amended), the Consumer Credit Act and the Unfair Contract Terms Act.

Trade Descriptions Act

The Trade Descriptions Act makes it a criminal offence:

- to make false statements about goods offered for sale
- to make misleading statements about services

Examples of offences therefore include:

- stating that a car for sale has clocked up 15,000 miles, when in fact the figure is 25,000 miles
- making a misleading statement about the price of goods, eg saying 'Now only £49.95, was £99.95' when it has only ever sold for £69.95
- making a misleading statement about a service, eg 'our dry cleaning is guaranteed to remove every stain' when it does not, or 'our apartments are within easy reach of the sea' when they are fifteen miles away

Sale of Goods Act 1979

This Act and subsequent amendments (including the Supply of Goods and Services Act 1982) state that you are entitled to expect any goods that you buy from a shop to be:

of 'satisfactory quality'
This means they must meet the standard that a 'reasonable' person would expect given the description and the price.

'fit for the purpose'
The goods must do what they are supposed to do, or what the shop claims they can do: an umbrella should keep the rain out, a watch should keep accurate time.

'as described'
The goods must be what they are claimed to be: a 'leather coat' must be made of leather, a 'surround sound cinema system' must provide surround sound.

If any of these three conditions is not met, the purchaser is entitled to a full or a part refund, depending on how soon the fault appears, how serious it is and how quickly the matter is taken up. Note also the following points:

- the buyer can accept a replacement, but can also insist on a refund if a replacement is not wanted
- the buyer does not have to accept a credit note for spending on other purchases
- a shop is not entitled to put up a notice saying "No Refunds!"

Consumer Credit Act 1974

The Consumer Credit Act regulates the majority of **credit agreements**, eg credit and store cards, personal loans and overdrafts. Its main aim is to prevent the consumer being 'ripped off' and pressurised into signing an unsuitable credit agreement. The consumer is given a variety of 'cooling off' rights, depending on where the agreement was signed and in whose presence.

The consumer is also protected by this Act which states that the seller of goods and services between £100 and £30,000 and the credit provider have 'equal liability' for breach of contract or misrepresentation. This means that if you buy goods or book a holiday using a credit card and the seller 'goes bust' you can claim from the credit card company for loss incurred.

If a business is in the retail sector, knowledge of this piece of consumer legislation is very important.

A credit agreement governs the following types of contracts:

- **Credit sale agreements** – ie finance options for the purchase of goods and services. This is basically a loan to cover the purchase price of the item, with the loan paid back in instalments over a period of months or years. The item is owned from the date the contract is signed.
- **Hire purchase (HP) agreements** – this is where the consumer pays monthly instalments to hire the item, but will not legally own it until the final instalment has been paid.
- **Hire agreements** – this is the hire of goods in return for a monthly payment. The consumer will never own the item, but must keep up the payments for the term of the contract to avoid having the goods repossessed and being sued for the outstanding debt.

Unfair Contract Terms Act

Any organisation that tries to insist on **unfair terms** (eg in small print on the back of a sales contract) may be in breach of the Unfair Contract Terms Act. This would protect, for example, holidaymakers who are not put up in the hotel they booked because the small print stated that the holiday company had the right to move them to another resort. This would be seen as an 'unfair term' and would enable the holidaymaker to seek compensation. In short, a business cannot 'contract out' through the small print.

It must be stressed that the terms must be 'unfair' in order to break the law. Terms and conditions on sales documentation are normally carefully worded so that they will stand up to examination in a court of law. Generally speaking, the supplier has the upper hand in dictating terms, as you can see on the contract excerpt on page 67.

We will describe the processes of taking court action for the recovery of debt in Chapter 6.

Late Payment of Commercial Debts (Interest) Act

This Act gives a supplier an automatic statutory right to claim interest from a customer when payment is withheld. See page 51.

Data Protection Act

This Act covers the protection of personal data about individuals held by organisations. See page 12.

Chapter Summary	■ Every time an organisation sells goods or services it enters into a contract – a legally binding agreement – with its customer. If the customer defaults on these terms, a breach of contract occurs which could be grounds for court action if the case is seen as being sufficiently serious.
	■ A contract has three elements: agreement, bargain and the intention to create legal relations.
	■ A breach of contract in the case of a contract for sale of goods or services lead to a court action for money compensation (action for price).
	■ The terms and conditions of the contract of sale are often set out on the back of sales documentation and may refer back to the original credit terms communicated to the customer when the account was opened.
	■ Sales of goods and services are also regulated by statute law, including the Trade Descriptions Act, the Sale of Goods Act, The Consumer Credit Act and the Unfair Contract Terms Act. An organisation is bound by this law and cannot contract out of its terms.

Key Terms

contract	a legally binding agreement enforceable in a court of law; it has three elements:
	1 an agreement, comprising an offer and an acceptance
	2 a bargain, ie value passing between the two parties (also known as 'consideration')
	3 an intention to create legal relations, ie a commercial agreement which could be taken to a court of law if the need arose
invitation to treat	an invitation to make an offer (eg catalogue, shop window) – not a contract
breach of contract	breaking of the terms of a contract and grounds for taking legal action
damages	money compensation for loss or injury
action for the price	taking legal action in the courts for recovery of an unpaid debt
retention of title	the right of a seller of goods to retain ownership of the goods until payment is made
Trade Descriptions Act	makes it a criminal offence for a seller to make false and misleading statements about goods and services
Sale of Goods Act	goods sold should be of satisfactory quality, fit for the purpose and as described by the seller
Consumer Credit Act	regulates credit agreements made by consumers, eg credit cards, personal loans and hire purchase – helps prevent pressure selling and provides cooling off periods
Unfair Contract Terms Act	
	regulates against unfair terms ('small print clauses') in contracts
Late Payment of Commercial Debts (Interest) Act	
	allows suppliers to charge interest on overdue amounts owing

Activities

4.1 The features which must always be present to create a valid contract are:

(a) offer, acceptance, consideration, specific performance

(b) offer, acceptance, bargain, retention of title

(c) offer, acceptance, consideration, expiry date

(d) offer, acceptance, consideration, intention to create legal relations

Which one of these options is correct?

4.2 Consideration in a contract is:

(a) taking advice before entering into a contract

(b) the promise by both parties to exchange value

(c) the need for both parties to have capacity to contract

(d) the intention to create legal relations

Which one of these options is correct?

4.3 An offer in a contract is:

(a) an invitation to treat

(b) the agreement of a fixed price

(c) a buyer signing a purchase order

(d) the price agreed for a purchase

Which one of these options is correct?

4.4 Carlo shops for sugar in a supermarket. A contract is formed when:

(a) he ticks the sugar off on his shopping list

(b) he takes the sugar off the shelf and puts it in his trolley

(c) he places the sugar on the checkout conveyor belt

(d) the checkout assistant scans the sugar and the price shows on the display

Which one of these options is correct?

4.5 Maria agrees to do some cleaning for her friend, Carlo, as a favour. After she has done the work he promises to give her £10 because he is so pleased with it. This constitutes a valid contract.

True or False? State your reasons for your answer.

4.6 K Hallett Ltd orders some goods from LFC Supplies but K Hallett Ltd fails to pay. LFC Supplies has the right under the contract to take K Hallett Ltd to court and sue for the money. This is known as:

(a) an action for the price

(b) retention of title

(c) an action for specific performance

(d) an intention to create legal relations

Which one of these options is correct?

4.7 A written contract that may be set aside because one of the parties was pressurised into signing it is known as:

(a) a void contract

(b) a voidable contract

(c) an unenforceable contract

(d) an illegal contract

Which one of these options is correct?

4.8 The Sale of Goods Act states that a buyer of goods should expect the goods to be:

(a) of satisfactory quality, fit for the purpose, sold at the price stated on the price ticket

(b) of satisfactory quality, fit for the purpose, sold at the price requested at the checkout

(c) of satisfactory quality, fit for the purpose, as described

(d) of acceptable quality, fit for the purpose, as described

Which one of these options is correct?

4.9 The Trade Descriptions Act makes it a criminal offence to:

(a) make a false or misleading statement about goods offered for sale

(b) make a false statement about the nature of your business

(c) sell goods that are less than satisfactory in quality

(d) sell goods that are not fit for purpose

Which one of these options is correct?

4.10 The Consumer Credit Act regulates the giving of credit references on customers.

True or False?

5 Monitoring and controlling customer accounts

this chapter covers...

In the last three chapters we described the credit assessment of customers and the opening of sales ledger accounts. In this chapter we move to the third stage in the credit control process (shown inside the dotted line on the next page) and explain how sales ledger accounts are monitored using various analytical techniques which include:

- *the receivables (aged debtors) analysis*
- *comparing customer accounts with average periods of credit*
- *the 80/20 rule*

Particular emphasis will be given to the receivables analysis which shows:

- *the extent to which individual accounts have debts outstanding*
- *average periods of credit given to sales ledger accounts as a whole*
- *the warning signs of accounts turning into doubtful and bad debts*

This chapter describes how debts are chased and customers are persuaded to pay on time, so helping the liquidity of the organisation. These procedures are carried out in line with an organisation's credit policy document.

This chapter also looks at alternative methods of collecting debts, including:

- *credit insurance (insuring against bad debts)*
- *factoring and invoice discounting (lending money against invoices issued)*

In the next and final chapter we pass on to the last stage in the credit control process and describe how an organisation deals with customers that will not or cannot pay invoices, either because they are short of cash, or because they are insolvent.

the credit control process

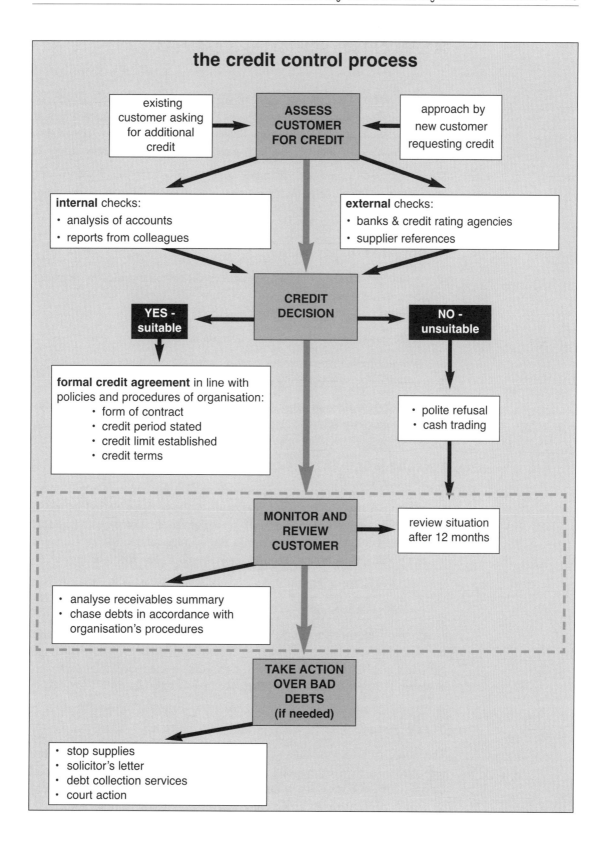

existing customer asking for additional credit

ASSESS CUSTOMER FOR CREDIT

approach by new customer requesting credit

internal checks:
- analysis of accounts
- reports from colleagues

external checks:
- banks & credit rating agencies
- supplier references

CREDIT DECISION

YES - suitable

NO - unsuitable

formal credit agreement in line with policies and procedures of organisation:
- form of contract
- credit period stated
- credit limit established
- credit terms

- polite refusal
- cash trading

MONITOR AND REVIEW CUSTOMER

review situation after 12 months

- analyse receivables summary
- chase debts in accordance with organisation's procedures

TAKE ACTION OVER BAD DEBTS (if needed)

- stop supplies
- solicitor's letter
- debt collection services
- court action

CREDIT CONTROL MONITORING TECHNIQUES

There are various techniques that can be used to monitor the accounts of customers. The main monitoring process is the **receivables analysis** which provides critical information about the accounts of individual customers. This is described in detail on the next page and the pages that follow.

There are also a number of other guiding principles and sources of information used in an effectively managed credit control function. These are described below.

trading history

As we saw in Chapter 3 the analysis of a credit customer relies to an extent on the customer's trading history:

- has the customer kept within the agreed credit limit?
- has the customer settled sales invoices on time?

This will tell the credit controller how reliable the customer is and whether the customer may need chasing up.

This can also, in case of any doubt, be backed up by the taking of **status reports** from credit reference agencies.

average periods of credit

In Chapter 2 we explained the use of performance indicators in credit rating a customer. A useful benchmark indicator is the average period of credit given to the receivables (debtors) of an organisation. This is calculated as **receivables turnover** – in other words, the average number of days it takes the receivables of an organisation to settle invoices. The formula is:

$$\frac{\text{receivables} \times 365}{\text{sales revenue}} = \text{average length of credit taken}$$

Therefore, if an individual customer given 30 days terms is taking 40 days on average to settle invoices and the receivables turnover is 50 days, then the customer may not give great cause for concern. If the receivables turnover, however, is 30 days, the account may well need investigation.

80/20 rule

The 80/20 rule in this context states that 80% of the total value of the receivables (ie 80% of the total of the sales ledger balances) is represented by only 20% of customers. It therefore follows that the organisation would do well to concentrate its credit control efforts on that 20% of customers.

materiality

It follows that the remaining 80% of customers (and 20% of the sales ledger balances outstanding) are not as **material** to the credit control process as the top 20% of customers.

You may well have studied **materiality** as an accounting concept. This states that certain amounts are of such low value that they are not worth recording. If a customer, for example, has an balance due of £5 on an account, possibly because of some mix up in calculating the amount paid, this will not be **material** and is unlikely to chased up, apart from the sending of a statement.

RECEIVABLES (AGED DEBTORS) ANALYSIS

receivables analysis and liquidity

A **receivables analysis** is a summary of amounts owed by customers, analysed into time period columns showing how long the amounts have been outstanding. It shows an organisation which of its customers are slow in settling invoices and which customers may become bad debts.

A receivables analysis is an essential report which pinpoints the cause of potential **liquidity** problems and is critical in the process of liquidity management. Funds not received from receivables are funds which will need to be financed from elsewhere and will increase the costs of the organisation.

format of a receivables analysis

A receivables analysis can either be drawn up **manually**, or it can be printed out as a report from a **computer accounting package**. There is no 'set' format for the receivables analysis, but the report normally follows the same columnar pattern.

An example of a computer printed receivables analysis from a computer accounting package is shown and explained at the top of the next page. An alternative spreadsheet version, showing percentages of the periods for which amounts have been outstanding, is shown at the bottom of the next page.

The **credit control policy** of the organisation will normally state when the receivables analysis should be produced. This is normally after the end of each month after the statements have been sent out. From the analysis the organisation decides which customers it is going to chase up, and how. It may send a letter or an email, or it may telephone the customer. Again, the credit control policy will set out guidelines for how and when communications should be sent.

The illustration below shows a receivables analysis (also known as an 'aged debtors analysis') produced as a report from the Sales Ledger in a proprietory computer accounting program.

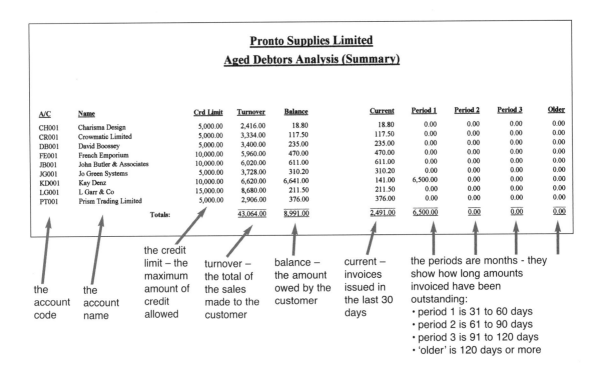

A receivables analysis can also be set out on a spreadsheet, as seen in the illustration below.

FAIRARM FOODS		RECEIVABLES ANALYSIS			31 July		
Account	Account number	Credit Limit	Balance	up to 30 days	31 - 60 days	61 - 90 days	91 days & over
Droof & Co	8721	1000.00	164.50	164.50	0.00	0.00	0.00
Flagand Ltd	8532	750.00	376.00	376.00	0.00	0.00	0.00
Granaro Supplies	8612	750.00	499.38	499.38	0.00	0.00	0.00
Les Gola Restaurant	7951	2000.00	1632.75	799.00	833.75	0.00	0.00
Romrod Designs	6025	2000.00	1926.88	380.00	0.00	1046.88	500.00
TOTALS			4599.51	2218.88	833.75	1046.88	500.00
Percentage			100%	48%	18%	23%	11%

how to use the receivables analysis

The columns of the receivables analysis on the previous page include:

- **account name and account number**

  Note that most receivables analyses will have more accounts than are shown here – possibly hundreds, shown in alphabetical order for ease of reference. This report is shortened for the purposes of illustration.

  The sales ledger account number is listed for reference purposes. In the case of the computer analysis, the account number is the computer account number allocated to the sales ledger account.

- **credit limit and balance columns**

  These two columns are compared to find out whether any customer is exceeding the allocated credit limit.

- **invoice 'age' columns**

  The remaining four columns here show how long the invoices which make up the total balance column have been outstanding.

Note that in the case of the second receivables analysis, the percentage outstanding for each period is shown in a row below the totals.

When analysing the report, the credit controller will look not only at individual accounts, but also at a number of relationships and trends by comparing this report with the previous month's analysis. For example, the percentages on the bottom row will indicate how quickly invoices are being settled. If percentages towards the right start to rise, there will be pressure on the company's liquidity, which will be seen in the company's bank balance.

Analysis of individual accounts is likely to start with a look at the far right-hand column. Are there any accounts with invoices which are well overdue? The £500 for Romrod Designs (second analysis), outstanding for over 91 days, could indicate a number of situations and will need to be investigated:

- the invoice (or invoices) might be subject to a dispute and remain unpaid

- extended credit may have been given on the invoice(s)

- Romrod Designs may be experiencing cash flow problems

This process will then continue as each column from right to left is scrutinised for 'out-of-order' amounts. Whatever the situation, action will need to be taken, in line with the Credit Control Policy.

Are there any accounts which are exceeding their credit limit? This will be picked up from a comparison of the credit limit and balance columns for each customer. Any excess of the limit will need to be investigated and action taken according to the guidelines in the Credit Control Policy.

It is normal practice for any action taken to be written on the report, eg 'send Letter 1 . . . telephone customer . . .threaten legal proceedings' and so on.

RECEIVABLES ANALYSIS – TAKING ACTION

Credit Control Policy

Most organisations will have a Credit Control Policy exists which sets out the procedures for chasing debts and guidelines for the timing of:

- invoices and statements of accounts sent to the customer
- production of the receivables analysis
- the making of telephone calls chasing overdue invoices
- the sending of emails or faxes chasing overdue invoices
- the sending of letters chasing overdue invoices
- setting up a meeting with the customer to discuss non-payment
- placing a customer on a 'stop' list, withdrawing further credit
- sending a letter threatening legal action
- taking legal action

An example of a Credit Control Policy is shown below. Note the instructions set out in the 'Debt Collection' section.

CREDIT POLICY & PROCEDURES

New Accounts	1	One bank reference and two trade references required.
	2	Analysis of minimum of three years' accounts for limited company customers.
Credit Terms	3	Standard terms 30 days from invoice. Any extension to be authorised by Credit Controller.
	4	2.5% settlement discount at Credit Controller's discretion.
Debt Collection	5	Invoices despatched on day of issue.
	6	Statements despatched first week of the month.
	7	Receivables analysis produced and analysed first week of the month.
	8	Reminder letter sent first week of the month for accounts 30 days overdue (Letter 1).
	9	Telephone chaser for accounts 45 days overdue. Meeting arranged if required.
	10	Customer on stop list if no payment received within 15 days of telephone chaser (unless meeting arranged). Sales Department notified.
	11	Letter placing account on stop and threatening legal action if payment not received within seven days (Letter 2).
	12	Legal proceedings set in motion if payment not received within 30 days of Letter 2 – subject to authorisation by Finance Director and notification of Sales Manager.

standard communications

The organisation is likely to have a set of standard **letters** which will vary in tone from the polite request for payment to the formal threatening of legal action. Even if the organisation does not have a written Policy, it is likely to have standard letters in its files. It is important that the standard letters are used as they will be designed to place the creditor (ie the issuer of the invoices) in a strong position should legal action become necessary. This is covered in full in the next chapter.

The **telephone** is a very efficient means of communicating a message and assessing reasons for non-payment. A letter can easily be put in a file and ignored, but a telephone call from a persistent creditor is difficult to ignore.

The chart below shows how an invoice can be chased. It is important to note that this is only an example and not a definitive method – different organisations will have different policies and processes.

We will explain the use of letters and the telephone in chasing debt in more detail in the pages that follow.

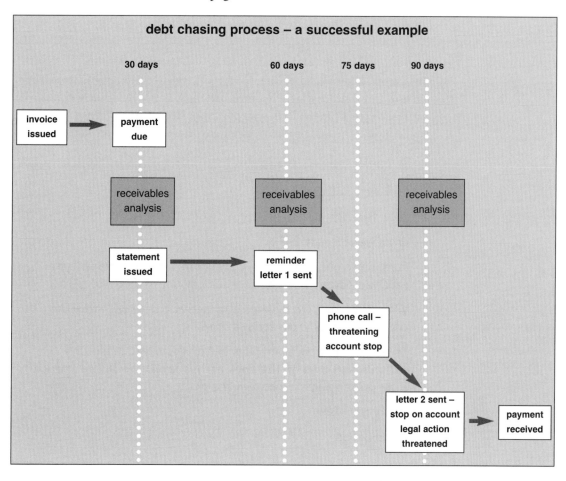

examples of letters

The first of the letter texts shown here is suitable for a 'Letter 1', ie the first chaser letter sent out (see item 8 in the Policy on page 80).

To Purchases Ledger

Dear Sir

Overdue Account 24122

We note from our records that your account balance of £10,456.50 is now overdue. The agreed payment terms are 30 days of invoice date.

Please settle this outstanding amount by return of post.

We attach an up-to-date statement.

Yours faithfully

Sales Ledger

The second letter would be suitable for a 'Letter 2' which places the account on stop and threatens legal action if payment is not received within seven days (see item 11 in the Policy on page 80). Note that the Sales Department would have to be told promptly about any account placed on stop.

To Purchases Ledger

Dear Sir

Overdue Account 24122

Further to our letter of . . . . we note that we have not yet received payment of the overdue amount of £10,456.50.

We regret that we have no alternative but to withdraw our credit facilities from today's date.

If we have not received payment of the overdue amount within seven days of the date of this letter we will commence legal proceedings to recover the debt.

Yours faithfully

Sales Ledger

using the telephone

The telephone is normally resorted to when statements and letters fail to have any effect. The telephone is a useful means of communication because it demands an immediate reply.

Organisations with a poor payment record will often come up with a variety of lame and blatantly untrue excuses on the telephone. It is the job of the person chasing the debts to have ready answers for all of these. A careful note should be made of all conversations. The table below provides some common examples of excuses and possible replies.

customer excuse	your response
'We have not received the invoice.'	'We will fax/email a copy today. Please let me know for whose attention it should be marked.'
	Comment: *A very common excuse. When sending a copy, ensure that it is addressed to the right person and is accompanied by a request for immediate payment.*
'There is nobody here to sign the cheque.'	'When will the authorised person be back? Are there any pre-signed cheques in the office?'
	Comment: *Do not accept the suggestion that there is unlikely to be anyone around to sign it for a while – there should always be someone who has been given suitable authority. If a signatory is going to be away for a long time, he/she will normally sign some blank cheques.*
'The cheque is in the post.'	'Please can you confirm to which address it was sent, and when?'
	Comment: *Oh yes? This excuse is so lame that it has become a standing joke. You will need to confirm the full details of the cheque and state a time limit for receipt before telephoning again and asking for a duplicate to be sent.*
'The computers are down.'	'Can you tell me when they are likely to be working again? Are you able to issue a hand-written cheque?'
	Comment: *A computer system that has failed will not be able to print out cheques. This is another lame excuse, although it is more likely to be true. You should insist that if the delay is an extended one (ie days rather than hours), the customer should write out a cheque by hand.*

receivables analysis – using discretion

It is important to appreciate that the debt-chasing actions carried out as a result of the monthly check through the receivables analysis should reflect the standing and payment record of each customer. Any Credit Control Policy cannot be relied upon to work 'by formula'.

For example, a **major customer** who accounts for a significant percentage of sales turnover and always pays up in the end will be treated with respect and will not necessarily be hounded for every overdue invoice. It is more likely that a diplomatic telephone call will achieve the desired result.

Conversely a relatively **small customer** with a poor payment record will be given less benefit of the doubt and will be pressed hard for overdue payments.

DOUBTFUL AND BAD DEBTS

Part of the job of the person working in credit control is to assess from the information to hand if a customer is going to default and not pay the balance due. The available information might include:

- **the receivables analysis** – the extent to which a customer's amounts owing are concentrated in the right-hand columns, ie to what extent they are overdue

- **internal information provided by the sales team** – they will know from visits and meetings if the customer bears the 'tell tale' signs of struggling financially, eg selling off assets, stockpiling, reducing the price of stock

- **internal information provided by the credit control staff** – the customer not responding to chasers, the customer providing poor excuses for non-payment, the customer's finance staff not taking telephone calls

- **comments from other organisations in the trade**, eg 'I know that ABC Limited is struggling' or 'I hear that ABC Limited staff wages are in arrears' or 'the ABC Limited MD has sold his Porsche'

doubtful debts

If a customer looks like he/she/it is going to default, the debt is said, for obvious reasons, to be '**doubtful**'. All this means is that the organisation, weighing up the probabilities, reckons that it is unlikely that it will get paid.

There is still a possibility that the money will come in, but it is 'doubtful'.

methods of making provision for doubtful debts

As you will know from your earlier studies, organisations adjust their accounting records by making **provision for doubtful debts** and setting the provision off against profits in a 'provision for doubtful debts account'. This provision is often **a set percentage**, eg 2%, of the total receivables, the percentage being based on experience within that type of organisation. If this method is adopted, the day-to-day running of credit control based on the receivables analysis will **not** be affected by the making of the provision.

Another method of making provisions for doubtful debts is to **carry out the process for individual debts** rather than relying on a percentage of total receivables. This means that each time the organisation assesses the receivables analysis, individual accounts which look unlikely to pay up are marked up for a doubtful debt provision, referred to management (eg the Credit Controller) and entered in a 'provision for doubtful debts account'. This is a less common method, largely because it is far more involved and time-consuming, but it is a method which features in assessments which require that you 'indicate accounts for which provision should be made.' This method is featured in the Case Study which follows.

dealing with bad debts

Bad debts are doubtful debts which have lost the element of doubt – it is considered by the organisation that they will definitely not be paid and will need to be written off in the accounts against profits in a 'bad debts written off account'. The treatment of bad debts and the situations which cause them are covered in detail in the next chapter.

Case Study

RENARD LIMITED: CREDIT CONTROL PROCEDURES

situation

You work as a credit control clerk for Renard Limited, a company that manufactures and sells brushes.

An extract from the company's Receivables Analysis and its Credit Control Policy are set out below, together with notes on the individual customer accounts.

You are to asked to write an email to Gordon White, Credit Controller, to

- analyse the situation of the four accounts in the receivables analysis
- recommend action that should be taken
- recommend whether any provision for doubtful debts should be made

Receivables Analysis					
Customer	Total due	1 - 30 days	31 - 60 days	61 - 90 days	91 days and over
Bruin Ltd	10,200.00				10,200.00
Ottaway Trading	4,100.00	2,340.00	950.00		810.00
R C Ratz	1,500.00		500.00	1,000.00	
S Quirrel	15,570.00	9,654.00	3560.00	2356.00	

CREDIT CONTROL POLICY (extract)

Debt Collection

1   Invoices to be issued on day goods are despatched.

2   Statements despatched first week of the month.

3   Receivables analysis produced and analysed first week of each month.

4   Reminder letter sent when a debt is 30 days overdue.

5   Telephone chaser for accounts when a debt is 45 days overdue.

6   Second letter and customer on stop list when debt is 60 days overdue and a meeting arranged with customer as soon as possible.

7   Letter threatening legal action is sent when debt is 90 days overdue.

8   Legal proceedings set in motion when debt is 120 days overdue, subject to agreement of Finance Director.

CUSTOMER BACKGROUND NOTES

Bruin Limited

No orders have been received from this customer for some months. No responses have been made to chaser letters. Telephone calls have been answered by the switchboard operator but the finance staff have always been unavailable.

Ottaway Trading

This account has been trading normally, but occasionally invoices have been overlooked or lost because of inefficiency. Reminder letters have been sent and a telephone call made about the £810 invoice, when the response was 'We will look into it.'

R C Ratz

Roland Ratz has been trading with you for a number of years and generally takes 60 days rather than 30 days to pay. Invoices have never been known to be outstanding for longer than 90 days.

S Quirrel

Sam Quirrel has only been trading with you for six months. He has a new business which is expanding rapidly. Last week he asked for an increase in his limit. He has not responded to earlier chasers.

EMAIL

to Gordon White, Credit Controller

from A Student

date today

subject Credit control: problem customers

Bruin Limited

This account gives cause for concern. They have ceased trading with our company. An invoice for £10,200 remains unpaid and has been outstanding for over 90 days. Indications are that the company is in financial difficulties. We should send our letter threatening legal action and bring the matter to the attention of the Finance Director. It would be worthwhile making enquiries in the trade if anything is known of this company's financial state. It is recommended that a provision for doubtful debts should be made for this debt.

Ottaway Trading

This account has always paid eventually. A telephone chaser should be made about the £950 short-term overdue amount and a definite date for payment agreed. The £810 may either be a lost or a disputed invoice. This must also be chased on the telephone and the problem resolved promptly. No provision for doubtful debts need be made.

R C Ratz

This is a good account which has been with us for a number of years. A reminder letter should be sent about the overdue amounts (£1,500) but no further action should be taken. No provision for doubtful debts need be made.

S Quirrel

This situation gives considerable cause for concern. It is very likely that this new customer is overtrading and financing his liquidity at our expense – by not paying invoices. His request for an increased limit would confirm this. He has therefore become a substantial credit risk. Recommended actions are to place the account on stop and demand repayment of the overdue £5916 by return. This should be set out in a formal letter. The due dates of the current invoices should be put in the diary and the amounts chased if not received on time. It is recommended that a provision for doubtful debts should be made for this debt. Sales Department should be notified of our action.

OTHER METHODS OF COLLECTING TRADE DEBTS

There are a number of financial services available to organisations which can help them with debt collection and the avoidance of bad debts. These services are provided by banks, insurance and other financial institutions. They will improve or safeguard the liquidity of the organisation, but at a cost. They include:

- **credit insurance** – insuring against the risk of non-payment, both in the UK and overseas
- **factoring** – employing a finance company to run the sales ledger and in some cases insure against bad debts
- **invoice discounting** – borrowing money against invoices

We will explain these in turn.

UK sales – credit insurance

Credit insurance replaces cash lost when a debt goes bad. Typical options include:

- **whole turnover insurance** – general (up to 90%) coverage in the case of receivable default (non-payment of debts)
- insurance limited to **key accounts** – up to 40 customers with up to 100% coverage
- **single account** insurance – 100% cover

Overseas credit insurance is also available to cover the risk of non-payment by overseas customers either through customer default or through political events.

Credit insurance is covered in full on page 52.

factoring

A factoring company lends money against the invoices received from receivables of the business, providing liquidity before the invoice due dates. The factoring company takes over the administration of the sales ledger. It will normally lend up to 90% of outstanding invoice amounts as soon as the invoice is issued and will pay the balance (less charges) when the receivable settles.

Factoring companies also provide an optional bad debt protection scheme – ie insurance against bad debts – known as '**non-recourse' factoring**, for which a further charge is payable.

Factoring without bad debt protection is known as '**recourse' factoring** – ie if a debt goes bad, recourse has to be made to the customer who will have to write off the bad debt.

invoice discounting

Here a finance house lends money against invoices issued to selected customers of the organisation, but the organisation continues to operate its own sales ledger and credit management system. As a result, the customers do not realise that the financing is being carried out.

The finance house will normally only be prepared to set up invoice discounting for an organisation which has good credit management procedures in place. The finance house will generally lend between 60% to 90% of the invoice value.

effect on liquidity management

The first of the three schemes described above – **credit insurance** – safeguards liquidity and avoids the danger of a substantial customer default, an event which could have a catastrophic effect on liquidity and profitability.

The other two schemes – **factoring** and **invoice discounting** – will improve liquidity because income from sales will be received sooner rather than later. The organisation will have a reduced working capital financing cost, but will also incur charges for the services.

The organisation will need to consider carefully the cost/benefit situation. For example, in a time of high interest rates, the early receipt of money from invoices could reduce interest costs considerably. In a time of low interest rates, the benefit might only be marginal because borrowing by way of overdraft would be relatively cheap and a viable alternative.

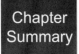

Chapter
Summary

■ There are a number of principles that can be used to monitor and control customer accounts. These include:

- examining the customer's trading history
- using the organisation's average credit period given to customers
- applying the 80/20 rule to the sales ledger
- using the concept of materiality
- analysing the receivables summary

■ The receivables (aged debtors) analysis is the report used by the credit control function to provide information about how long amounts have been outstanding on each customer account. It can also show total amounts outstanding on the sales ledger by percentage over different time periods. There are normally columns in the analysis for:
- customer name
- customer account number
- credit limit
- the balance of the account
- different time periods for amounts outstanding

■ The receivables analysis is regularly produced either as an automatic report from a computer accounting program or as a manual calculation from the accounting records.

■ Most organisations will have a Credit Control Policy which gives guidelines for the actions to be taken with customer accounts which have become overdue.

■ Letters are useful in the formal process of debt collection, although they can easily be ignored by the customer. Letters are normally standardised and graded according to the seriousness of the situation.

■ Telephone calls, when used with skill, cannot be ignored and are a persuasive means of chasing overdue amounts. The person telephoning should have replies ready for the usual excuses for non-payment.

■ The standing and payment record of each customer should also be borne in mind when chasing debts. The receivables analysis cannot be relied upon as the sole source of information about the customer.

■ Credit insurance is available for UK sales, either for the whole of the sales ledger, or for a group of key accounts, or for single accounts. Credit insurance for exports is also available for overseas sales.

■ Factoring companies lend money against receivables' invoices, either with bad debt cover (non-recourse factoring) or without bad debt cover (recourse factoring). The factoring company manages the sales ledger.

■ Invoice discounting involves lending money against invoices, but the organisation keeps control of its sales ledger.

■ Credit insurance, factoring and invoice discounting can all help to improve liquidity, but the cost of these schemes must be taken into account when deciding whether to use them.

Key
Terms

average period of credit	the average period of credit given to the customers of an organisation; this is measured in days by the receivables turnover formula:

$$\frac{\text{receivables (debtors)} \times 365}{\text{sales revenue}}$$

80/20 rule	the rule that about 80% of the total value of customer accounts outstanding will be represented by about 20% of the customer accounts
materiality	the accounting concept that states that insignificant amounts should be disregarded
receivables analysis	a summary of amounts owed by sales ledger customers, analysed into columns, showing how long the amounts have been outstanding
credit control policy	a document drawn up by an organisation which sets out procedures for managing the sales ledger, including actions to be taken in order to chase outstanding debts, eg letters, telephone calls and legal proceedings
doubtful debt	a sales ledger debt which is unlikely to be paid – but there is still the chance that it may be paid; a provision may be made in the accounts for the debt
bad debt	a sales ledger account which is written off in the books against profit
credit insurance	an insurance policy which covers the possible loss of money through a customer defaulting on payment, ie loss through a bad debt
export credit insurance	special insurance to cover the risk of non-payment by overseas customers either through customer default or through some political event
factoring	a service managing the sales ledger of another organisation and lending money against the organisation's invoices
invoice factoring	a service lending money against an organisation's invoices, but allowing the organisation to continue to operate its own sales ledger and credit management

Activities

5.1   The 80/20 rule applied to credit control states that:

(a)   80% of customers are normally a good credit risk and 20% will need stricter credit control

(b)   about 80% of the total value of all the customers' accounts is accounted for by about 20% of the customers

(c)   an organisation should concentrate its credit control policy on 80% of the customers, the remaining 20% normally being a good credit risk

(d)   if a customer account becomes a bad debt, 80% of that amount can be written off against profits

Which one of these options is correct?

5.2   Which of the following is a list of techniques which are likely to be used in credit control?

(a)   receivables analysis, 80/20 rule, comparison with average payables turnover period

(b)   receivables analysis, materiality, statement of cash flows

(c)   receivables analysis, 80/20 rule, comparison with average receivables turnover period

(d)   receivables analysis, 80/20 rule, statement of cash flows

Choose the correct option.

5.3   A receivables (aged debtors) analysis is:

(a)   a summary of customers that have been trading with a business for over 10 years

(b)   a summary of small debts that have been outstanding for over 12 months and may have to be written off

(c)   an analysis of supplier accounts based on the amounts outstanding and the period for which they have been outstanding

(d)   an analysis of customer accounts based on the amounts outstanding and the period for which they have been outstanding

Which one of these options is correct?

5.4   Invoice discounting is:

(a)   a loan provided by a finance company against invoices issued to customers

(b)   a loan provided by a finance company to the buyer against invoices issued by a supplier

(b)   the provision of settlement discount on customer invoices

(d)   writing off an invoice which has become a doubtful debt

Which one of these options is correct?

5.5 The extract below from the receivables analysis of Dowzee Limited shows the total amount outstanding and the period totals.

Standard terms are payment 30 days after invoice date.

The company does not have a written Credit Control Policy.

The company does not have any standard chaser letters but instead relies on sending out statements every month and making telephone calls to slow payers.

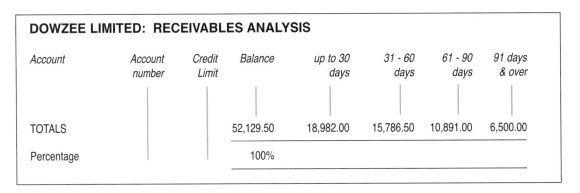

DOWZEE LIMITED: RECEIVABLES ANALYSIS

Account	Account number	Credit Limit	Balance	up to 30 days	31 - 60 days	61 - 90 days	91 days & over
TOTALS			52,129.50	18,982.00	15,786.50	10,891.00	6,500.00
Percentage			100%				

You are to:

(a)   work out the percentages (to the nearest percentage) of each period total

(b)   explain the effect of the situation on the liquidity of the company

(c)   identify any problems with the credit control of the company

(d)   suggest solutions to the problems

5.6 You are debt chasing at the beginning of the month and have a list of customers to telephone. Some of them are co-operative and agree to settle overdue amounts straightaway, but some are less helpful.

How would you deal with the following situations which all relate to amounts that are over one month overdue?

The Credit Control Policy states that a telephone chaser should be made in each case and payment by return of post requested.

(a)   The customer says 'I think the cheque was posted to you yesterday, so should be with you today or tomorrow.'

(b)   The customer says 'the cheque is waiting for signature, but the line manager who has to sign it is off sick with a bad back.'

(c)   The customer says 'Sorry, but we don't seem to have received this invoice.'

(d)   The customer says 'this is in hand but our cheque issuing is now computerised and the next payment run is in ten days time in the middle of the month.'

5.7 An extract from the receivables analysis for S Freud Limited as at 30 November is shown below, together with details of payments received from receivables and invoices issued during November.

An extract from the Credit Control Policy of S Freud Limited is also shown below.

S Freud Limited – Receivables Analysis as at 30 November					
Customer	Total due	1 - 30 days	31 - 60 days	61 - 90 days	91 days and over
Karl Young & Co	7,500.00				7,500.00
Fred Neesher	6,095.00	5,095.00	1,000.00		
J Bentham	499.00	100.00		399.00	

S FREUD LIMITED – CREDIT CONTROL POLICY (extract)

- One month's credit allowed from date of invoice.

- Statements despatched on first working day of the month.

- Receivables analysis produced at the beginning of each month.

- Reminder Letter 1 sent when account is 31 days overdue.

- Telephone chaser made when account is 45 days overdue.

- Reminder Letter 2 sent when account is 61 days overdue. This threatens legal action and account stop if payment not received within 7 days.

- Account stop and legal proceedings to be instigated and provision for doubtful debts to be made if payment not received as a result of Letter 2.

You are to:

(a) State how discussion should be conducted with any overdue accounts.

(b) Write an email dated 30 November to Ivor Pound, Credit Controller, setting out the actions which should be taken with each of the three customers (in line with the Credit Control Policy), including any recommendations for doubtful debt provision. Use your own name.

5.8   You work in the credit control section of Moore Trading Limited, a wholesaler.

You regularly review the main accounts of the business to ensure that they are trading within their limit and pay their invoices on time.

The main documents you work from are:

- the Credit Control Policy document (CCP) for Moore Trading Limited

- the monthly Receivables Analysis

- the list of credit limits

- notes on the customer accounts compiled from the Sales Ledger section and your own previous dealings

These are all set out on the next three pages.

You are to

(a)   Review the Receivables Analysis, also using the credit limit list.

(b)   Review the customer account notes.

(c)   Draft action points on each of the ten main accounts. These should be suitable for an email to be sent to the Credit Controller.

The plan should, for each case

- identify the customer

- analyse the current position

- suggest a course of action (if required) including any doubtful debt provision or bad debt write-off that may be necessary

CREDIT CONTROL POLICY FOR MOORE TRADING LIMITED

Current credit control procedures following the agreement of a credit limit:

1.   An order for goods is received by email, fax or phone (all phone calls are recorded).

2.   Goods are delivered and a goods received note is signed by the customer.

3.   The goods received notes are kept in a file in the accounts office.

4.   An invoice will be issued a few days after delivery on 30 day terms.

5.   An analysis of trade receivables is produced monthly.

6.   A reminder telephone call is made when the debt is 14 days overdue.

7.   When a debt is 30 days overdue a standard chaser letter is sent.

8.   When the account is 60 days overdue the account will be put on stop.

9.   If the debt is 90 days overdue, it will either be placed in the hands of a debt collection company or legal proceedings may be instigated if the customer does not respond to calls or letters. The debt will be classified as a doubtful debt.

10.   If the customer becomes insolvent (bankruptcy, administration, liquidation) the account should be stopped (if not already stopped) and the amount of the debt fixed and classified as a doubtful debt. Investigations should be made about any goods supplied as the title may remain with Moore Trading Limited. This is in accordance with the standard retention of title clause in the Moore Trading Limited terms and conditions issued to all customers.

MOORE TRADING LIMITED: RECEIVABLES ANALYSIS AS AT 31 MARCH					
	Balance £	**0 – 30 days** £	**31 – 60 days** £	**61 – 90 days** £	**Over 90 days** £
Customer					
Al Binoni Ltd	20,000	20,000			
B Rahms & Co	55,000				55,000
CIM Arosa Ltd	65,000	30,000	35,000		
H Umell	60,000	60,000			
L Garr & Co	65,000		20,000	20,000	25,000
Mendell & Son	(20,000)	(20,000)			
G Reeg	45,000				45,000
B Britten Ltd	40,000	20,000	20,000		
E Whittaker Ltd	90,000	30,000	30,000	30,000	
V Williams & Co	30,000	20,000	10,000		

Customer Credit Limits	
	£
Al Binoni Ltd	40,000
B Rahms & Co	50,000
CIM Arosa Ltd	60,000
H Umell	90,000
L Garr & Co	40,000
Mendell & Son	45,000
G Reeg	20,000
B Britten Ltd	40,000
E Whittaker Ltd	75,000
V Williams & Co	40,000

Notes on the ten main customers of Moore Trading Limited

1   Al Binoni Ltd, a new customer with a limit of £40,000 placed its first order a few weeks ago. A new order for £15,000 of goods has just been received.

2   B Rahms & Co have not responded to any chaser letters or telephone calls. The credit limit is £50,000

3   CIM Arosa Ltd is a new customer and was given a credit limit of £60,000. There was a report in the local paper that the company has had to make 20% of its staff redundant. CIM Arosa Ltd has just placed an order for another £10,000 of goods.

4   H Umell is a long standing customer and has always settled the account within trading terms.

5   L Garr & Co has gone into administration. The account is not credit insured.

6   The account of Mendell & Son is in credit because they have duplicated a payment.

7   G Reeg is not responding to any communications.

8   B Britten Ltd is a new business with a limit of £40,000. The company has just placed an order for £30,000 of goods but no payment has yet been made on the account.

9   E Whittaker Ltd is a long established customer and has always paid eventually, but has a history of late payment. Moore Trading's Limited's Managing Director recently agreed to extend the terms of the account to 60 days. The account limit is £75,000.

10 V Williams & Co has been purchasing £20,000 or less per month. The limit is £40,000.

6 Collecting debts and dealing with insolvency

this chapter covers...

In the last chapter we described the credit control process in action and explained the use of the receivables (aged debtors) summary and other internal records as the basis for taking action to recover money owing from receivables.

In this chapter we take the process a stage further and describe how organisations attempt to recover amounts which the customer either will not or cannot repay. This involves a number of stages and options:

- *ensuring that there is a valid debt and underlying contract on which to base any action*

- *using debt collection agencies to recover the debt*

- *using a solicitor to recover the debt*

- *taking the customer to court to recover the debt on the basis of the contract of sale*

- *taking the customer through the insolvency courts and dealing with customers who are already insolvent*

Publisher's note: accounting and legal terminology

You will be well aware of the effect of the introduction of International Accounting Standards on accounting terminology. For example a **debtor** (UK terminology) = a **receivable** (International terminology) and a **creditor** (UK terminology) = a **payable** (International terminology)

You should also appreciate that **legal terminology** uses the term 'debtor' for a person who owes a debt and the term 'creditor' for a person who is owed a debt. The terms 'debtor' and 'creditor' are used occasionally in this chapter, but in the strictly legal sense.

BAD DEBTS – THE FINAL FRONTIER

doubtful and bad debts

In the last chapter we saw that a **doubtful debt** is a debt that is **unlikely** to be paid and will have to be provided for in the accounts. A **bad debt**, on the other hand, is a debt that will **definitely not** be paid and will have to be written off in the accounts to the income statement as an expense to the business.

is it worth it?

A bad debt is the final stage in the credit control process. It occurs when the organisation gives up trying to recover the debt and decides to minimise its losses by writing it off through the income statement.

As we will see in this chapter, as the debt recovery process moves to the stage where debt collection agencies, solicitors or court action are involved, the costs start to mount up. The question has to be asked 'is it worth it?' This can happen when:

- the debt is relatively small when compared with the cost of recovery
- the customer looks like becoming insolvent (unable to pay debts)
- the customer is insolvent (a bankrupt individual or company in liquidation)

It must be remembered that an organisation is only likely to recover a debt – even through court action – if the receivable (debtor) has the money or other realisable assets to enable the debt to be repaid. To use a common phrase, there is no point 'flogging a dead horse.'

If you are working in credit control you may have to recommend bad debts for writing off. The Credit Control Policy may allow you to write off small debts (say up to £100), but you will need to refer larger amounts to the Credit Controller.

is there a contract of sale?

A **contract** is the legal agreement which should support all sales transactions. This does not mean that there has to be a formal written document relating to every invoice – a contract can be oral (word of mouth), but there does have to be an agreement which involves:

- an offer for sale and an acceptance of the offer, eg when an order is placed by a customer
- value changing hands both ways (eg money and goods at an agreed price)
- the realisation by seller and buyer that the agreement has legal consequences and could end up in court if the agreement is broken

Please see Chapter 4 (pages 66-67) for further details of commercial contracts.

The important point here is that if a debt is to be pursued through legal channels including solicitors and the courts, there must be a valid contract relating to it.

If the customer can show that there is no contract, the organisation has no hope of being able to recover the money. The following are examples of 'no hope' situations:

- the customer has not signed an order form where the order form is the agreement to purchase
- the goods or services have been supplied, but have not been ordered
- an order has been cancelled by the customer by email before goods were despatched

breach of contract

Legal action can be taken against a customer when a contract is in existence because non-payment is a **breach of contract** – the customer is not carrying out an agreed part of the bargain.

There are a number of **remedies** available for breach of contract in a wide variety of situations. The remedy chosen will depend on the type of contract. For example, a builder who is contracted to build a house and disappears off site before putting the roof on, can be ordered by the court to complete the work (the remedy of **specific performance**). If, however, the person having the house built refuses the builder access to the site, the builder could **terminate** the contract and demand payment for what had been done (the remedy of **quantum meruit**, which means 'what it deserves').

These situations do not have much in common with credit control in an organisation. Here the remedy of **action for the price** – ie taking legal action in the courts for recovery of an unpaid debt – is the normal remedy for breach of contract.

USING THIRD PARTIES FOR COLLECTING DEBT

When an organisation finds that its own credit control process is proving unsuccessful in getting customers to pay up, it can employ third parties, such as **debt collection agencies** and **solicitors**, to try and recover debts.

debt collection agencies

Debt collection agencies are commercial organisations that collect debts on behalf of clients. They are normally paid by taking a percentage of the amount collected. In other words, the more successful they are, the more they receive – which is a major incentive for being successful. They tend to be effective at debt collecting because after a while customers tend to ignore the credit control letters and telephone calls of the supplier, but when an independent body is called in to collect debt, they take more notice and are more likely to pay. Debt collection agencies have a distinct psychological advantage.

A typical debt collection schedule follows a number of steps in quick succession until payment is received:

Day 1	Send a chaser letter to the customer.
Day 4	Telephone the customer.
Day 12	Telephone the customer again.
Day 20	Send a letter threatening legal action.
Day 28	Start legal proceedings – suing for the debt in the courts.

Debt collection agencies can achieve a success rate of around 70%. The organisations that employ them should carefully monitor their success rates to ensure that they are operating efficiently.

solicitors

Customers do not like receiving letters from solicitors chasing debts and threatening legal action in the courts. A solicitor's letter is therefore often an effective way of recovering a well-overdue invoice.

When employing a solicitor for this purpose it is important to use a firm that specialises in debt collection. Solicitors are not cheap, nor will the Small Claims Court (see next page) reimburse solicitors' costs, so they should only be used when there is a reasonable chance of the customer being able to repay the debt. It is also important to be precise when providing the solicitor with details of the debt and customer, eg the exact amount owed, the name and address of the customer. Any mistake might invalidate the claim.

TAKING THE CUSTOMER TO COURT

There are two ways in which a debtor (customer) may be taken by to court:

- to **enforce repayment of the debt** – assuming that the customer is solvent and can repay debts when they are due; this is the most common form of court action taken as part of the credit control process
- to bring about the **bankruptcy** (of an individual) or **liquidation** (of a limited company) – assuming that the debtor (customer) is insolvent and is unable to repay debts when they are due and hoping that some money will be realised from the customer's assets; this is a last resort action and is not often taken as part of the credit control process

We will look first at the process of taking the customer to court to enforce payment of the debt.

the court system – amounts of claim

The County Court deals with claims by payables and offers three 'tracks':

- **Small Claims Court** if the claim for recovery of debt is £5,000 or less; this has the advantage that you do not have to use a solicitor or barrister – you can present the case yourself if you wish
- **Fast Track** applies to more serious cases, for claims between £5,000 and £15,000
- **Multi-Track** is for more complex cases, normally over £15,000

The **High Court** deals with claims over £25,000. Most claims for repayment of debt are dealt with in the main County Court and the Small Claims Court.

When completing the paperwork for the claim to the court it is vital that details such as identifying the receivable and the debt are correct, eg:

- the name of the individual or the company
- the address of the individual or the company
- the amount owing
- the date of the debt

When the paperwork has been lodged, the court will issue a 'default summons' to the customer who can either agree to the claim (which is unlikely), ignore it (in which case judgement will go against the customer) or go ahead with the court proceedings.

the court system – what happens if you win

If the County Court or Small Claims Court decision goes in the favour of the payable, a County Court Judgement will be issued against the receivable.

The customer will either pay up, in which case the debt is repaid and all is well, or the customer will refuse to pay, either because he/she does not want to, or because he/she does not have sufficient assets to repay the debt.

One initial option to persuade the customer to pay up is a court order for an **oral examination**. The customer is required to come to court to be questioned on details of income, capital and savings. This procedure is likely to put pressure on the cross-examined customer to pay the payable the money due; this is because the customer should have revealed, under oath, the money or realisable assets that are available to repay the debt.

enforcement of the judgement

If the customer does not pay up it will be necessary to apply to the court for enforcement of the judgement so that the debt can be repaid in full, or (more likely) in part.

There are a number of options open to the payable who wishes to enforce judgement by court order:

garnishee order	This is a court order which the payable can have sent to a third party who owes money, requiring the money to be paid direct to the payable. A common example of the third party is a bank or building society which has an account for the receivable. The order will claim the due amount from the bank or building society account of the receivable on that day. This will only work if the money is in the account. If the account is low in funds or overdrawn, the payable will get little or nothing. It is all a question of timing and knowing when money has been paid in.
warrant of execution	This order is a request for the court bailiffs to enter the receivable's home or business premises to seize belongings or assets to sell and pay off the debt. The restrictions here are that the bailiffs are not allowed to break down the door or to seize essential living items or 'tools of the trade'.
warrant of delivery	If the receivable has goods which belong to the payable (for example goods sold and covered by a 'retention of title' clause), the payable can obtain a court order – a 'warrant of delivery' – which will give the court bailiffs authority to obtain and collect the goods.

attachment of earnings   If the receivable is working and earning, an Attachment of Earnings Order may be granted by the court. This will require the receivable's employer to deduct a certain amount from the receivable's salary on a regular basis until the debt is repaid. The judge will decide on the proportion which can be deducted, as the receivable will money for living expenses.

charging order   If the receivable owns property the payable can apply to the court to 'register a charge' on the property to show that the payable has an interest in the money received from the eventual sale of the property. This is more of a 'last ditch' defence and can run into major problems if the receivable has family and children who will be made homeless if the property is sold.

Of these court orders, the warrant of execution (sending in the bailiffs) and attachment of earnings (deduction from salary) are the most reliable and most common remedies.

If all else fails, the payable can resort to the insolvency courts to bring about the sale of the receivable's assets and the distribution of the money realised to **all** of the payables. This is described in detail on the next page.

'NO HOPE' DEBT OR BAD DEBT?

It is important to repeat at this point that it is only worth a trade payable taking a customer to court and enforcing a court order if the customer has funds and other assets available to repay the debt. Note that the term 'trade payable' refers to a commercial ('trade') organisation which sells goods or services on credit and does not take any security for the debt.

More often than not an overdue debt will be the result of a customer running into serious financial difficulties, in which case no amount of costly court action will produce any results.

No available assets means no repayment.

The solution in this case is to write the amount off as a bad debt in the accounts, where at least the amount can be set off through the income statement against the tax liability of the organisation.

We look further at this type of situation in the Case Study on page 109.

CUSTOMERS AND INSOLVENCY

the insolvency process in a nutshell

insolvency is being unable to pay debts as they fall due

A payable – the '**creditor**' – such as a trading business can take a receivable to court to prove that the receivable – the '**debtor**' – is insolvent. The result of this is that the court will then arrange for the receivable's assets to be sold off and **all** the payables repaid as far as is possible with the money realised by the sale. It is unlikely that the payables will get all their money back – trade (unsecured) payables are often at the back of the queue for repayment and may receive little or nothing. The insolvency process for trade payables is therefore a last resort and money owed very often ends up as a bad debt.

some legal terminology

The laws that cover insolvency and all its complexities are:

- **Insolvency Act 1986**, which has been amended to some extent by
- **Enterprise Act 2002**

Further information can be found at the very helpful official website www.insolvency.gov.uk

The law is never straightforward and so there are some terms to remember:

An individual (eg sole trader or partner in a partnership) who is proved by the court to be insolvent becomes a **bankrupt**.

The individual normally remains a bankrupt for 12 months, after which he/she is discharged, although arrangements to repay debt from earnings may run for a further two years.

A limited company that is proved by the court to be insolvent is said to be **in liquidation**. A limited company cannot therefore be said to be 'bankrupt'.

the stages of the insolvency process

Suppose you run a business and a major customer of yours – a sole trader – will not pay up. You wish to make them bankrupt. The stages are:

1   Ensure the debt is £750 or more (a lower amount is not sufficient for the bankruptcy process).

2   Make a 'statutory demand' to the receivable on an official form for the amount owing.

3   If payment is not received within three weeks, send in a 'creditors petition' to the court. A meeting of all creditors may be called by the

court. Creditors will be asked to send in a statement ('proof') of what they are owed by the receivable.

4   The court makes a bankruptcy order against the receivable (the 'debtor') and appoints an official (the 'trustee in bankruptcy') who arranges the sale of the receivable's assets (except domestic items and tools of the trade) and distributes the money to the payables in the following order of priority:

- the costs of the bankruptcy proceedings (ie court costs and fees)

- preferential debts (items such as employee wages)

- any floating charge holder (eg a bank which has a secured overdraft)

- unsecured payables such as trade payables (ie you)

You will see from this that trade suppliers of a bankrupt individual are last in the list to be paid off. What little remains after court costs, employee wages and the secured bank overdraft have been paid off in full, has then to be shared proportionally between trade suppliers. So if, for example, trade suppliers are owed £50,000 and there is only £5,000 left, they will get a 'dividend' of only 10p in the £. They may be lucky to get this.

Note also the following:

• Trade suppliers who do not start the insolvency process themselves will be advised by the court when bankruptcy proceedings are under way and will be asked to send in a statement of what they are owed; they will be kept informed of the progress of the proceedings and will receive any 'dividend' in due course.

• The process for putting limited companies into liquidation follows very much the same pattern, except that the shareholders of the company will be the last in the queue for repayment of their investment from the proceeds of the sale of assets.

administration and administrative receivers

The law is not always helpful in its choice of terminology. The terms **administration** and **administrative receivers** are a case in point. They both relate to areas of insolvency where the interests of trade suppliers are not looked after particularly well, but they relate to very different situations.

1 **Administration** is a state of affairs where an organisation which is running into solvency problems has an **administrator** appointed by the court to run its affairs. When an organisation is in administration – football clubs sometimes seem to fall into this category – no other payable can petition for bankruptcy or liquidation. The organisation is protected from payables, including the bank.

2 The other situation involves a bank which has the security of a floating charge over the assets of a company to secure its overdraft. The security document enables the bank to appoint an **administrative receiver** to sell the secured assets of the company. In this situation the unsecured payables will again be practically last in the queue for repayment while the bank will be able to maximise the amount it receives.

In the Case Study that follows we look at a variety of situations which involve recommendations and decisions which have to be made within the Credit Control function relating to:

- debt collection

- court action

- insolvencies

- provision for doubtful debts and bad debt write offs

Case Study

WESSEX LIMITED:
DEALING WITH PROBLEM ACCOUNTS

situation

You work as a credit control clerk for Wessex Limited, a company that manufactures high quality garden furniture.

At the end of the month you are asked to deal with the receivables analysis and sort out any queries relating to problem sales ledger accounts.

The main queries you have been presented with are set out below. You have been asked to:

- state what action you would take in each case

- suggest where provision for doubtful debts is to be made

- indicate if any debt is to be written off as a bad debt

You are to set out your recommendations in an email to the Credit Controller, Tom Hardy.

1   Slow paying accounts

You note from the recent receivables analysis that five accounts are more than 90 days overdue (standard terms are payment at the end of the month following the invoice date). None of the accounts is responding to your letters and telephone calls. All of the accounts have just been sent a letter threatening legal action.

Tom Hardy, the Credit Controller, has commented to you "There's no point taking these accounts to court – we do a lot of business with them and they are probably basically sound. They just need a lot of encouragement to make them pay up, a letter from a debt collection agency, for example."

2   **Wildeve Limited – disputed transaction**

Wildeve Limited has a history of being an awkward customer. There is currently £1,200 more than 90 days outstanding. Your investigations show that this amount relates to a shipment of chairs which Wildeve Limited claims was not ordered. You look through your copy sales invoice file and cannot trace a purchase order or any record of how the order was placed. The latest email from the customer says "You can come and collect the goods if you wish. They are still in their original packing. You will be liable for the carriage costs."

Tom Hardy asks "Shall we call in our solicitor?"

3   **John Newson – County Court debtor**

You have successfully obtained a County Court judgement against John Newson for non-payment of a debt for £6,000. John Newson is a salaried purchasing manager for a chain of garden centres and has also been running a sole trader business as a landscape designer 'on the side'. You believe he has substantial assets, but he is refusing to pay, even after the court judgement.

Tom Hardy asks "What can we do to get this man to pay?"

Suggest two suitable methods of enforcing the judgement.

4   **Ken Everdene – bankruptcy order**

Tom Hardy brings you an official letter which is notification of a bankruptcy order made against your customer Ken Everdene. You check the account balance and your receivables analysis and find that Ken owes a total of £4,500 represented by invoices spread over a 30 to 90 day period.

5   **Stourminster Consultancy Limited – notice of Administration**

You have been worried about the account of Stourminster Consultancy Limited which has been overdue to the extent of £1,750 for a couple of months. You have heard from local reports that the business has been having problems in meeting its commitments. You now receive notice that it has been placed in Administration.

solution

Please see the email on the next page.

EMAIL

to   Tom Hardy, Credit Controller

from   A Student

date   today

subject Credit control: problem accounts

1   **Slow paying accounts**
    I recommend the employment of a debt collection agency. The accounts are likely to be stirred into action and make payment when the pattern of debt chasing changes and accelerates. It would be too costly and inappropriate to employ a solictor at this stage when there is a reasonable likelihood of the money being paid. No provision for doubtful debts needs to be made yet.

2   **Wildeve Limited – disputed transaction**
    Unfortunately in this case there is no evidence of an order, which is the acceptance of our offer for sale, and so there is no valid contract. Unless evidence can be found, we will be liable for collection of the goods and will have to cancel the invoice. We cannot sue where there is no contract.

3   **John Newson – County Court debtor**
    Enforcement of the court judgement could be made either as an attachment of earnings (the receivable has a salary from his employer) or as a warrant of execution (sending the bailiffs in). Other remedies such as garnishee order, warrant of delivery or charging order will not be so effective. Provision for doubtful debts needs to be made at this stage.

4   **Ken Everdene – bankruptcy order**
    The bankruptcy order indicates that bankruptcy proceedings have commenced against this customer. We will have to complete a proof of debt form for the court, listing the invoices totalling £4,500. It is doubtful if we will receive much of a dividend, but provision for doubtful debts needs to be made at this stage. This may well become a bad debt at a later stage.

5   **Stourminster Consultancy Limited – notice of Administration**
    The fact that this company has been placed in Administration means that payables such as ourselves can do very little apart from carry out our usual debt chasing procedures. We are unable to take any legal action or consider insolvency proceedings. It would be wise to make provision for doubtful debts at this stage.

A Student

■ The credit control function of an organisation may decide to use a third party such as a debt collection agency or a solicitor to chase up debts. These third parties can often exert more pressure on a customer than the supplier.

■ The credit control process of an organisation must assess whether the process of debt collection through legal action can be justified in terms of the size of the debt and the likelihood of recovering the debt.

■ It is important that a valid contract underlies all sales transactions. If legal action is to be taken to recover a debt there must be a contract on which to sue the receivable.

■ An organisation can take a receivable to court either to enforce repayment of debt or to bring about the bankruptcy of an individual or the liquidation of a company.

■ A County Court judgement requiring the receivable to repay the debt owing is the most common outcome of legal action taken by the credit control function of an organisation.

■ If the receivable does not repay the debt after judgement has been made in the payable's favour, the payable can obtain a court order to enforce repayment. The most common of these are warrant of execution (using bailiffs to seize assets) and attachment of earnings (deduction from salary).

■ Taking court action to bring about the bankruptcy or liquidation of a receivable is another way of obtaining repayment of some element of the debt outstanding.

■ Bringing about the bankruptcy or liquidation of a receivable in the courts will result in all the assets of the receivable being sold off and distributed (in principle) to all the payables.

■ The distribution of the sale proceeds of the assets in a bankruptcy or liquidation of a receivable is made in a strict order of priority: court costs and fees, preferential payables, floating charge holders and then unsecured trade payables. Payables who are owed money on invoices are therefore last in the list and may receive little or no money.

■ The credit control function of an organisation must know about the effect of alternatives to the normal insolvency route – for example administrations and the appointment by secured payables (such as a bank) of administrative receivers. These alternatives significantly weaken the position of a trade payable.

Key Terms		
	doubtful debt	a sales ledger debt which is unlikely to be paid
	bad debt	a sales ledger account which will not be paid and is written off in the books against profit
	contract	an agreement between two parties which must involve an offer and acceptance, the passing of value by both parties and the intention that it can form the basis of legal action if the need arises
	breach of contract	breaking of a term (or terms) of the contract which can be remedied through taking legal action in the courts
	receivable/debtor	the individual or organisation who owes the money – against whom court action may be taken
	payable/creditor	the individual or organisation who is owed the money – and who takes court action
	action for the price	taking legal action in the courts for the recovery of an unpaid debt
	debt collection agency	a commercial organisation which collects debts for third parties
	Small Claims Court	a 'fast track' court for less complex cases, including suing for recovery of debts under £5,000; the case does not need to involve a solicitor or barrister and can be brought by the payable in person
	oral examination	a court order requiring the receivable to be cross examined in court to provide details of assets – used when the receivable refuses to pay up
	garnishee order	a court order claiming money from a third party (eg a bank account) which is owed to the payable
	warrant of execution	a court order authorising the bailiffs to seize the assets of a receivable who refuses to pay up
	warrant of delivery	a court order authorising the bailiffs to seize assets belonging to the payable but held by the receivable

attachment of earnings   a court order requiring an employer to deduct a proportion of the receivable's earnings and pay it to the payable

charging order   registration of a charge (interest) in a property belonging to the receivable which entitles the payable to be paid part of the money received for the property when it is sold

insolvency   being unable to pay debts as they fall due

bankruptcy   the situation where an individual (eg sole trader or partner) is taken to court and proved to be insolvent so that his/her assets can be sold and distributed to payables

liquidation   the situation where a limited company is taken to court and proved to be insolvent so that its assets can be sold and distributed to payables

statutory demand   a formal written demand to the receivable from the payable demanding repayment of a debt (at least £750) within 21 days; a necessary condition for the bankruptcy/liquidation process

trade creditors/payables   commercial organisations that supply goods and services on credit and on an unsecured basis – often the last to be paid off in insolvency proceedings

preferential creditors   payables such as employees who are owed wages by the receivable and who will be paid off in priority to trade payables

administrative receiver   an individual appointed under a floating charge (bank security) to sell the assets of the receivable when the security is called in; this ensures that the bank will be paid in priority to the trade payables

administration   arrangement whereby a receivable running into solvency problems has an administrator appointed by the court to run its affairs; while an administrator is in place no payable can take legal action to recover debts

Activities

6.1   A customer could refuse payment of an invoice for goods supplied by claiming that there is no valid contract when:

(a)   the supplier has not offered settlement discount terms on the sales invoice as the supplier normally does

(b)   the customer has not signed the purchase order which has been issued in the first place

(c)   the supplier has dropped the price of the goods supplied following the placing of the order

(d)   an administration order has been placed on the supplier

Which one of these options is correct?

6.2   When a customer is in breach of contract for non-payment the supplier will normally pursue the following remedy:

(a)   an action for the price

(b)   an action for specific performance

(c)   an action for 'quantum meruit'

(d)   an action for termination of the contract

Which one of these options is correct?

6.3   When a supplier wishes to claim in the courts for a customer debt of £2,500, the route he/she should take would be:

(a)   the High Court

(b)   the Multi-track system

(c)   the Fast Track system

(d)   the Small Claims Court

Which one of these options is correct?

6.4   An enforcement of a court judgement on a customer which involves the allocation and payment to the supplier of money on the bank account of the customer is known as a:

(a)   warrant of execution

(b)   warrant of delivery

(c)   garnishee order

(d)   charging order

Which one of these options is correct?

6.5 A supplier that wishes to place a statutory demand to instigate the bankruptcy process on a customer must submit a claim for an amount owing that is at least:

(a)   £500

(b)   £750

(c)   £1,500

(d)   £5,000

Which one of these options is correct?

6.6 You work in a credit control department and receive notice that your customer Furbo Limited, who owes £5,000, has been placed in administration. You should:

(a)   pursue the debt in the normal way

(b)   petition for the company's bankruptcy

(c)   obtain a warrant of delivery

(d)   obtain a warrant of execution

Which one of these options is correct?

6.7 An Administrative Receiver is the official appointed by the court to run the affairs of a company which has been placed into administration.

True or False?

6.8 You work for Bishop Imports which is owed £5,000 by Dodge E Trading Limited, which has recently been put into liquidation.

You receive a schedule from the court stating that £400,000 has been realised by the sale of the company's assets. The creditors (payables) that are paid out of this sum are :

- liquidation costs of £85,000

- preferential payables of £127,000 (employee wages)

- Midwest Bank floating charge to cover the company's overdraft £150,000

- Unsecured trade payables of £190,000 (including the £5,000 owed to Bishop Imports)

(i) The dividend per £1 owed that should be paid to Bishop Imports is therefore:

(a) 76p

(b) 100p

(c) 80p

(d) 20p

(ii) The amount that will be received by Bishop Imports is ....

Answers to activities

CHAPTER 1: INTRODUCTION TO CREDIT CONTROL

1.1 (b)

1.2 (a)

1.3 (c)

1.4 (d)

1.5 (b)

1.6 (c)

1.7 (a)

1.8 (a) Company financial details (accounts); payment record, details of directors, records of any insolvency proceedings.

  (b) Advantages: speed of response, reliability of information, comprehensive information. Disadvantages: cost, possibility that some information may be out of date.

1.9 Unless GML Importers has written authority from its customer to release information, to do so would be a breach of the duty of confidentiality and also of the Data Protection Act 1998 which protects the rights of 'data subjects'. The request should be politely declined.

1.10 Letter to Bart Attman, Director, Toppo Toys Limited, address as letterhead. Text should acknowledge their request and politely ask for bank reference (plus authority for bank) and two trade references, while at the same time acknowledging current cash trading. See page 6 for similar letter. References will still be required because there is a need to comply with the Credit Policy Manual.

CHAPTER 2: FINANCIAL ANALYSIS OF CUSTOMER ACCOUNTS

2.1   (a)   The bank reference is qualified by the word 'should', which can be translated as 'not always' and sounds a warning note of caution.

     (b)   Both trade references are also qualified, using the words 'normally' (B Ruckner Ltd) and 'usually' (V Williams). This again means 'not always' and indicates that Stylo Limited can be late payers. Note also that both suppliers allow 60 days, which indicates that late payment can be very late (see payable days figure in [c] below).

     (c)   See table below.

	Year 1	**Year 2**	**Year 3**
Current ratio	1.06:1	1.07:1	1.03:1
Liquid capital ratio	0.76:1	0.74:1	0.61:1
Receivable days	43	43	48
Payable days	60	63	65
Net profit %	2.67%	1.92%	1.94%
Interest cover	1.33	1.21	1.18
Gearing	58.9%	59.5%	63.5%

     (d)   Comments on performance indicators:

Liquidity

The *current* and *liquid capital* ratios are well below the ideal of 2 : 1 and 1 : 1 respectively and give cause for concern about the ability of the company to be able to settle its liabilities on time.

Receivable days show that debtors are taking an increasingly long time to settle and provide the much needed cash, although the period of 43 to 48 days in not unusual.

Payable days show that the company is taking increasingly long credit, which would concern any new supplier.

Profitability

Net profit % is running at a dismally low level and gives no confidence in the company's continuing ability to generate cash.

Interest cover shows that operating profit is barely covering interest payments. Any increase in borrowing or in interest rates could make the company's liquidity vulnerable.

Financing

Gearing is high and is increasing, indicating too much reliance on borrowing.

     (e)   Stylo Limited, by all indication, is a dubious credit risk, with a known record of late and long payment and tight liquidity.

The application should be politely declined and cash trading suggested for a trial period (6 months) to see how the relationship develops. If there is pressure from management in other areas of the business to take on Stylo Limited for reasons of expediency, a lower limit (eg £7,500) and thirty days credit (Policy Manual) should possibly be offered, and the account monitored very closely to ensure that the terms are adhered to.

2.2 (a) & (b)

Customer: De Gass Limited	Indicator	Score
Operating profit margin %	16.5%	10
Interest cover	7.86	10
Current ratio	1.5 : 1	0
Gearing %	38.71%	10
Total score		30

Customer: Vangov Limited	Indicator	Score
Operating profit margin %	4.8%	0
Interest cover	2.28	0
Current ratio	1.27 : 1	0
Gearing %	72.73%	− 20
Total score		− 20

(c)   The level of credit risk of De Gass Limited is very low and that of Vangov Limited is medium.

(d)   De Gass Limited can be considered good for a limit of £50,000

(e)   The accounts of Vangov Limited indicate a number of weaknesses.

- Profitability is low, with operating profit at only 4.8%, covering interest only 2.28 times

- Liquidity is also vulnerable, with the current ratio at only 1.27 : 1. Also, inventory is high at £2m, and if taken out of current assets, gives a liquid capital ratio of only 0.29 : 1 which shows that the company may have difficulty in meeting its current liabilities.

- Financial position is also questionable with gearing high at 72.73%

CHAPTER 3: GRANTING CREDIT AND SETTING UP THE ACCOUNT

3.1   (d)

3.2   (b)

3.3   (a)

3.4   (c)

3.5   (b)

3.6   (a)

3.7   (c)

3.8   (a)   27 May   (b)   30 June   (c)   2 June

3.9   (a)   18.53%

(b)   (i)   No. The figure is higher than the cost of borrowing and therefore unattractive.

(ii)   Yes. The figure is lower than the cost of borrowing and therefore attractive.

3.10   (a)   Year 1: 35

Year 2: – 20

(b)   Year 1: Very low risk

Year 2: Medium risk

(c)   The internal policy documentation states that the proposition must be referred to the Financial Director. As the score is – 20 and only 5 points off being a high risk and unacceptable, the recommendation is likely to be a refusal with the proviso that trading on a cash basis could be suggested.

(d)   A possible text could run as follows:

'Thank you for your application form dated .... requesting a credit limit of £45,000.

We have assessed your application for credit using our usual criteria and have taken up references, but very much regret that we are unable to offer credit facilities to you at present.

We very much value your custom and would be very pleased to trade with you on a cash basis for the time being and then review the situation after, say, six months.

We look forward to hearing from you.

A Student'

3.11   (a) & (b)

Performance indicator	Year 2	current
Profit from operations margin %	15.32%	32.00%
Interest cover	2.1	8
Current ratio	1.03 : 1	2 : 1
Gearing %	65.22%	46.67%

Conclusion:

The trends of all four performance indicators are very positive and will greatly reduce the level of credit risk, meaning that a positive recommendation may be given to the Finance Director for the increase in credit limit from £50,000 to £90,000.

Comments on performance indicators:

Profit from operations margin has increased from 15.32% to 32.00%. The percentage has more than doubled which means that the company is generating more profit which in turn should improve liquidity.

Interest cover has increased from just over 2 to 8 times. The profit from operations provides excellent cover for interest costs, which again indicates higher liquidity.

Current ratio which is a direct indicator of liquidity, has improved to a very comfortable 2 : 1, with a cushion of liquidity equal to the extent of the current liabilities.

Gearing has dropped from 65.22% to below 50% which indicates that the company is now less reliant on external financing – and the interest cost of covering that financing – which means that an increase in the credit limit becomes less of a credit risk for RPG Limited.

(c)   The text of the email should include the following:

–   a summary of the recent trading history, including trading within the existing limit and settling invoices in line with the 30 day terms

–   a summary of the improvement shown in the financial accounts, possibly using the table produced in (a) above as a basis, highlighting the improved liquidity of Hermes Limited

–   a firm recommendation for an increase in limit from £50,000 to £90,000

CHAPTER 4: RUNNING THE ACCOUNT – LEGAL CONSIDERATIONS

4.1   (d)

4.2   (b)

4.3   (c)

4.4   (d)

4.5   False. The agreement was not set up with the intention to create legal relations.

4.6   (a)

4.7   (b)

4.8   (c)

4.9   (a)

4.10 False. The Consumer Credit Act regulates credit agreements such as hire purchase and personal loans granted to consumers.

CHAPTER 5: MONITORING AND CONTROLLING CUSTOMER ACCOUNTS

5.1 (b)

5.2 (c)

5.3 (d)

5.4 (a)

5.5 (a)

DOWZEE LIMITED: RECEIVABLES ANALYSIS							
Account	Account number	Credit Limit	Balance	up to 30 days	31 - 60 days	61 - 90 days	91 days & over
TOTALS			52,129.50	18,982.00	15,786.50	10,891.00	6,500.00
Percentage			100%	36%	30%	21%	13%

(b)   The liquidity of the company will be restricted as a result of the overdue accounts. Note that only 36% of the total outstanding is within the limit. 30% is over 30 days overdue and 34% over 60 days overdue. This situation may also conceal some potential bad debts which, should they materialise, will reduce liquidity on a permanent basis.

(c)   Problems can be identified as the lack of a formal Credit Control Policy, the lack of standard chaser letters and any structure for reinforcement of debt collection.

(d)   Solutions would be to rectify this lax situation. This would involve the drawing up of a formal Credit Control Policy, the drafting of standard chaser letters and the establishment of procedures for debt collection.

5.6   The replies should be along the following lines, and made politely:

(a)   'We have not received the cheque yet. Please would you confirm the address to which it was sent and whether it was sent first or second class post.'

(b)   'Is there anyone else who can sign it in place of the line manager? Do you have a pre-signed cheque which you could use?'

(c)   'We will send a copy invoice to you today. Would fax or email be preferable? Please can you let us know for whose attention it should be marked.'

(d)   'This cheque is now overdue. Please could you send us a hand-written cheque by return of post.'

5.7   (a)   Overdue accounts should be dealt with firmly and politely. In case of doubt, reference should be made to an authorised person within the company. Due regard should be made to the status of the customer and flexibility exercised where necessary – for example: is the account important to the business? is there pressure from Sales Department to increase sales, even if invoices are settled late?

(b)   The email to Ivor Pound should deal with the three customers as follows:

Karl Young & Co
The £7,500 owed by Karl Young & Co is now over 91 days overdue. The customer will have received Letter 2 threatening legal action after 61 days. If no acceptable reason for non-payment has been received, the account should be stopped, provision for doubtful debts made and legal proceedings instigated.

Fred Neesher
Letter 1 should go out when the £1,000 is more than 31 days outstanding. The situation should be monitored and a telephone chaser made during the month if payment is not received. No provision for doubtful debts need be made at this stage.

J Bentham
This account seems to be taking 60 days credit as a matter of course. If this extension to the normal 30 days has not been authorised, the customer should be sent a Letter 2 and the situation monitored carefully. No provision for doubtful debts need be made at this stage.

5.8   **Note:** References 'CCP" are to the Credit Control Policy Document of Moore Trading Limited.

1   This is satisfactory trading from Al Binoni Ltd and so no action need be taken.

2   As B Rahms & Co have not responded to any letters or call, the debt should be placed in the hands of a debt collection company or legal proceedings could be instigated (CCP 9)

3   The CIM Arosa Ltd account is over the limit by £5,000. The report in the local paper suggests that the company is having financial problems. Further investigations should be made. No credit should be allowed for the order for £10,000 and the outstanding amount should be chased by letter. (CCP 7)

4   H Umell. No problem – a account with a good record, no action needed.

5   L Garr Ltd is in administration and not covered by credit insurance. The account should be stopped, no further dealings should take place and investigations made about stock held by L Garr Ltd which may be claimable by a retention of title clause. The account should be marked as a doubtful debt.

6   Mendell & Son should be sent a statement showing them the credit balance on the sales ledger account.

7   As G Reeg is not responding to any communications the debt should be placed in the hands of a debt collection company or legal proceedings could be instigated (CCP 9). If it has not already been done the account should be marked as a doubtful debt.

8   The order for £30,000 placed by B Britten Ltd will place the customer unacceptably beyond the limit of £40,000. The customer should be contacted by phone and a request made for the settlement of the account without delay before any further sales can be made. (CCP 6)

9   The E Whittaker Ltd account is standing at £15,000 above the limit and payment is late for the £30,000 due within 60 days. However the account has a satisfactory history of payment and the confidence of the Managing Director, so should not give cause for any action apart from the sending of a statement.

10   V Williams & Co. No problem – no action needed.

CHAPTER 6: COLLECTING DEBTS AND DEALING WITH INSOLVENCY

6.1 (b)

6.2 (a)

6.3 (d)

6.4 (c)

6.5 (b)

6.6 (a)

6.7 False. An Administrative Receiver is normally appointed under a floating charge over a company's assets. A company in administration continues to run as normal with full use of its assets, but under the control of an Administrator appointed by the Court.

6.8

(i)

(d) Workings:

Realisation of assets		£400,000
Less		
Liquidation costs	£85,000	
Preferential payables (wages)	£127,000	
Floating charge holder	£150,000	
		£362,000
Available for unsecured payables		£38,000
Dividend £38,000/£190,000		20p in £

(ii) £1,000

Workings: £5,000 x 20p

AAT Sample Assessment

Credit management and control

This Sample Assessment has been provided by the Association of Accounting Technicians and is reproduced here with their kind permission.

The Sample Assessment is in two parts:

1   A computer-based assessment completed online (page 128)

2   A Case Study Project to be submitted online (page 134)

AAT's answers to both are provided, starting on page 143.

Publisher's note — accounting terminology

UK accounting terminology is used in this sample Assessment. AAT has stated that at present UK and international terminology may be used interchangeably in this Learning Area. You will find that the terminology used by Osborne Books in this book is also interchangeable but predominantly international, in line with the Learning Area 'Financial Statements'.

Credit Management and Control

Section 1 – Online assessment

1.1 The essential features of a valid simple contract are:

    A.   Offer, acceptance and consideration only

    B.   Offer, acceptance, consideration, intention to create legal relations and certainty of terms only

    C.   Offer and acceptance only

    D.   Offer, acceptance, intention to create legal relations only

1.2 Consideration is:

    A.   The intention of the parties to be legally bound

    B.   The need for fairness in the contract

    C.   The promise to exchange value

    D.   The payment of cash

1.3 Mohammad orders a pizza by telephone, and says he will pay on delivery. Which of the following would constitute consideration?

    A.   Calling the pizza restaurant

    B.   Handing over money to the pizza delivery person

    C.   Accepting delivery of the pizza

    D.   Promising to pay for the pizza

1.4 Dave shops at a supermarket. A contract is formed when:

    A.   Dave pays for his shopping

    B.   Dave puts his selection in the trolley

    C.   The checkout assistant takes Dave's goods

    D.   Dave picks up items from the shelves

1.5 Mary is the owner of a florist. She places a notice in the window advertising the sale of roses at half price. The notice is:

    A.   A contractual offer

    B.   A completed contract

    C.   An acceptance of an offer

    D.   An invitation to treat

1.6 Alpha Limited receives a letter from Beta Limited containing an order for 100 kilograms of rice. Alpha sends Beta a schedule of standard conditions which includes the clause that payment is due within 30 days of invoice date. This clause is an example of:

A.   An invitation to treat

B.   Consideration

C.   An offer

D.   A misrepresentation

1.7 John receives a letter from Michael containing an order of 50kg of sugar for £100. Which of the following statements is correct?

A.   Michael's letter is an invitation to treat and John's response that he can supply the sugar is an offer

B.   Michael's letter is an offer and John's response that he can supply the sugar is an acceptance

C.   Michael's letter is an acceptance and John's response that he cannot supply the sugar is a breach of contract

D.   Michaels' letter is an acceptance and John's response that he can supply the sugar is consideration

1.8 Mary orders some clothing which is advertised as being 100% pure new wool. When she receives the goods, the label says 60% wool and 40% Polyester. Mary has a claim for breach of contract due to:

A.   Fiduciary misconduct

B.   Misrepresentation

C.   Misuse of Sales Act

D.   Unfair Contract Terms Act

1.9 The Late Payment of Commercial Debts (Interest) Act allows:

A.   Customers to charge interest on overdue amounts owing

B.   Commercial banks to charge interest on loans

C.   Suppliers to charge interest on overdue amounts owing

D.   Suppliers to give discounts for early payment

1.10 Nita asks Harry for a price to paint the interior of her flat. Harry says he can do it for £200 and Nita says that will be fine. Halfway through the work Harry asks for an additional sum of £100 because he underestimated the work. Which of the following statements are correct?

A.   Nita must pay Harry the £100 because the agreement was made in good faith and Harry made a mistake

B.   Harry cannot force Nita to pay the additional amount because the agreement was for £200

C.   Harry can force Nita to pay because she never accepted the price

D.   If Nita refuses to pay Harry can simply work until he has done £200 worth of painting

2.1   The Data Protection Act applies to:

A.   Data about individuals only

B.   Data about individuals, companies and government departments

C.   Data about companies only

D.   Data about individuals and companies only

2.2   The Data Protection Act applies to:

A.   All records held by the company

B.   Only manual records

C.   Only computer records

D.   Only records of opinions

3.1   Company Alpha has a customer, Beta limited, who refuses to pay an outstanding amount of £500. Which of the following courts will deal with any action taken by Alpha to enforce the repayment of the debt?

A.   The High Court

B.   An Industrial Tribunal

C.   A Small Claims Court

D.   The County Court

3.2   Legal action can be taken against a customer for non payment of an invoice when:

A.   There is a contract in existence and the non payment is a breach of contract

B.   There is no contract in existence but the payment is still due

C.   There is a contract in existence and the non payment is a misrepresentation

D.   There is a contract in existence and the non payment is a remedy

3.3   The normal remedy for breach of contract due to non payment of the debt is:

A.   An action for specific performance

B.   An action for price

C.   An action for remedy

D.   An action for the goods

3.4   Retention of title is:

A.   The right of the purchaser to retain ownership of the goods received

B.   The right of the seller to retain ownership of the goods until a cheque has been posted

C.   The right of the seller to retain ownership of the goods until payment is made

D.   The right of the purchaser to expect that title is retained by the seller even when payment has been received

3.5   In order to petition the court for a winding up order, the company must be owed at least:

A.   £75

B.   £750

C.   £7,500

D.   £1,000

4.1   Why is liquidity management important?

A.   Liquidity management is important to ensure that a company does not make a loss

B.   Liquidity management is important so that the shareholders can see how much return they will get on their investment

C.   Liquidity management is important so that the company can estimate how much cash is tied up in stock and fixed assets

D.   Liquidity management is important so that the company can ensure that cash is available to discharge commitments

4.2   Alpha Limited has sold goods on credit to Beta Limited. The following information is available.

(i)   Aged debtor analysis

(ii)   Copies of outstanding invoices

(iii)   Copies of contractual documents

(iv)   Copies of trade references

(v)   Copies of bank references

Which of the above documents will be needed to aid the collection of the outstanding amounts owed by Beta Limited?

A.   All items

B.   (i), (ii) and (iii) only

C.   (i), (iv) and (v) only

D.   (iv) and (v) only

4.3 Which of the following information could be used to assess the credit status of a new customer?

(i) Financial accounts

(ii) Aged debtor analysis

(iii) Copies of outstanding invoices

(iv) Draft contract for trade

(v) Trade references

(vi) Bank references

A. All items

B. (i), (ii) and (iii) only

C. (i), (iv) and (v) only

D. (i), (v) and (vi) only

4.4 Which of the following is not a method of analysing credit control information?

A. Aged creditor analysis

B. Trading history

C. 80/20 rule

D. Materiality

4.5 The 80/20 rule method of analysing information on debtors is:

A. A rule where you only look at the first 80 customer records

B. A rule that 20 customers out of every 100 will go into liquidation

C. A rule that approximately 80% of the value of the amounts owed will be represented by approximately 20% of the customer accounts.

D. A rule that the company must make at least 20% profit out of every £100 of goods sold.

5.1 Which of the following is a reason for offering discounts for prompt payment?

A. To make the customer feel that they have received a bargain

B. To improve the cash flow of a business

C. To make more profit

D. To decrease the cost of loans

5.2   A company's terms of payment are 28 days. It is offering a discount of 5% for payment within 14 days. Customer A owes £1,000. Calculate the amount A will pay if they take advantage of the discount and also the simple annual interest rate of the discount.

    A.   £950, and 136.84%

    B.   £950 and 36.84%

    C.   £950 and 130%

    D.   £950 and 30%

6.1   Invoice discounting is a method where:

    A.   Discounts are given for early payment of invoices

    B.   A finance house lends money against invoices issued

    C.   A reduction is given for faulty goods

    D.   A judgement given by a court

6.2   Credit insurance allows a company to claim for:

    A.   Amounts owed by a customer who has defaulted on payment

    B.   Amounts owed to a bank on a mortgage

    C.   Amounts owed to creditors when a company makes losses

    D.   Amounts owed to shareholders when a director has acted illegally

6.3   Organisations often use debt collection agencies because:

    A.   Debt collection agencies have more powers than ordinary companies

    B.   Debt collection agencies can place customers on stop with all other suppliers in the sector

    C.   Debt collection agencies have a right to seize goods from customer

    D.   Debt collection agencies get results because customers take more notice and are more likely to pay

Section 2 – Online Project

(a) You work as a credit control manager for Alpha Limited which uses a credit rating system to assess the credit status of new and existing customers.

The credit rating (scoring) system table below is used to assess the risk of default by calculating key indicators (ratios), comparing them to the table and calculating an aggregate score.

CREDIT RATING (SCORING) SYSTEM	Score
Operating profit margin	
Losses	−5
Less than 5%	0
5% and above but less than 10%	5
10% and above but less than 20%	10
More than 20%	20
Interest cover	
No cover	−30
Less than 1	−20
More than 1 but less than 2	−10
More than 2 but less than 4	0
More than 4	10
Liquidity ratio	
Less than 1	−20
Between 1 and 1.25	−10
Between 1.25 and 1.5	0
Above 1.5	10
Gearing (total debt/(total debt plus equity))	
Less than 25%	20
25% and above but less than 50%	10
More than 50% less than 65%	0
Between 65% and 75%	−20
Between 75% and 80%	−40
Above 80%	−100
Risk	**Aggregate score**
Very low risk	Between 60 and 21
Low risk	Between 20 and 1
Medium risk	Between 0 and −24
High risk	Between −25 and −50
Very high risk	Above −50

New customer request form

The sales department has asked for a credit limit of £50,000 to be given to X Limited who is a potential new customer. The financial information below has been supplied by X Limited.

Accounts for X Limited	2009	2008
	£'000	£'000
Turnover	4,500	5,500
Cost of sales	3,500	3,800
Gross profit	1,000	1,700
Distribution costs	1,050	1,150
Administration costs	1,000	1,000
Operating profit	−1,050	−450
Interest payable	100	50
Profit on ordinary activities before taxation	−1,150	−500
Tax on profit on ordinary activities	0	0
Profit for the financial year	−1,150	−500
Balance sheet	**2009**	**2008**
	£'000	£'000
Fixed Assets		
Tangible assets	2,200	2,500
Current Assets		
Stocks	900	750
Trade Debtors	1,000	850
Cash	50	400
	1,950	2,000
Creditors amounts falling due within one year		
Trade creditors	2,100	1,800
Net current assets	−150	200
Creditors amounts falling due after more than one year		
Long term loans	1,000	500
Net assets	1,050	2,200
Capital and reserves		
Share capital	200	200
Profit and loss account	850	2,000
Shareholders' funds	1,050	2,200

New customer request form

The sales department has asked for a credit limit of £30,000 to be given to Z Limited who is a potential new customer. The financial information below has been supplied by Z Limited

Accounts for Z limited	2009	2008
	£'000	£'000
Turnover	9,000	8,000
Cost of sales	6,250	6,000
Gross profit	2,750	2,000
Distribution costs	850	850
Administration costs	600	600
Operating profit	1,300	550
Interest payable	250	250
Profit on ordinary activities before taxation	1,050	300
Tax on profit on ordinary activities	350	100
Profit for the financial year	700	200
Balance sheet	**2009**	**2008**
	£'000	£'000
Fixed Assets		
Tangible assets	4,500	3,900
Current Assets		
Stocks	1,200	1,000
Trade Debtors	700	600
Cash	400	400
	2,300	2,000
Creditors amounts falling due within one year		
Trade creditors	1,500	1,300
Net current assets	800	700
Creditors amounts falling due after more than one year		
Long term loans	2,500	2,500
Net assets	2,800	2,100
Capital and reserves		
Share capital	100	100
Profit and loss account	2,700	2000
Shareholders' funds	2,800	2,100

TASKS: PART (a)

1.1   Using the templates provided:

   (i)   Calculate the key indicators for 2008 and 2009 for X Limited and Z Limited, and

   (ii)   Rate each company using the credit rating (scoring) system.

1.2   Based on the results of your credit rating, recommend, with reasons, whether the requested credit limits should be given to X Limited and Z Limited.

1.3   Where credit is being refused, draft a note or a letter communicating the decision and explaining what action the company could take to improve its chances of being granted credit in the future.

   or . . .

   Prepare a telephone script which could be used by the person contacting the company to communicate the decision regarding the requested credit limit.

Template for Part (a) calculations:

X Limited Year	Indicator 2009	Rating	Indicator 2008	Rating
Operating profit margin				
Interest cover				
Current ratio				
Gearing				

Z Limited Year	Indicator 2009	Rating	Indicator 2008	Rating
Operating profit margin				
Interest cover				
Current ratio				
Gearing				

Existing customer requesting increased credit limit.

Y Limited has been trading with Alpha Limited for several years and has, until recently, always paid to terms. Following several late payments they have now contacted Alpha Limited to request an increase in their credit limit from £50,000 to £100,000. Y Limited has supplied the accounts below.

Accounts for Y limited	2009	2008
	£'000	£'000
Turnover	6,500	6,000
Cost of sales	4,600	3,800
Gross profit	1,900	2,200
Distribution costs	850	850
Administration costs	600	600
Operating profit	450	750
Interest payable	500	250
Profit on ordinary activities before taxation	-50	500
Tax on profit on ordinary activities	0	150
Profit for the financial year	-50	350
Balance sheet	**2009**	**2008**
	£'000	£'000
Fixed Assets		
Tangible assets	7,050	4,350
Current Assets		
Stocks	1,200	550
Trade Debtors	1,300	800
Cash	100	300
	2,600	1,650
Creditors amounts falling due within one year		
Trade creditors	2,100	1,400
Net current assets	500	250
Creditors amounts falling due after more than one year		
Long term loans	5,000	2,000
Net assets	2,550	2,600
Capital and reserves		
Share capital	100	100
Profit and loss account	2,450	2,500
Shareholders' funds	2,550	2,600

Additional information supplied by the sales department after a visit to Y Limited:

Y Limited has recently acquired several new large customers and therefore purchased new assets with long term loans to ensure that forecast sales demands can be met. The contracts with the new customers were only completed in the second half of the year, and it is expected that sales will continue to increase in 2010 with little increase in costs because the new machines have resulted in a reduction in variable cost per unit. The directors of Y Limited expect a profit after tax in 2010 of around £500,000. In anticipation of orders for 2010, Y Limited significantly increased its stock levels at the end of 2009.

Required

1.4 Using the templates provided:

(i) Calculate the key indicators for 2008 and 2009 for Y Limited, and

(ii) Rate the company using the credit rating (scoring) system.

1.5 Based on the results of your credit rating, and taking into account the trading history and additional information supplied by the sales department, recommend a course of action.

You could make use of additional terms in the contract or any other options open to Alpha limited which could provide additional comfort.

Template for Part (a) calculations:

	Y Limited _Year_	**Indicator** _2009_	**Rating**	**Indicator** _2008_	**Rating**
Operating profit margin					
Interest cover					
Current ratio					
Gearing					

PART B

You have been provided with the credit control policy for Alpha Limited, and an aged debtors' analysis at 31 March 2010. See below and on the next page.

CREDIT CONTROL POLICY FOR ALPHA LIMITED

Current credit control procedures once credit limit has been agreed:

1. An order for goods is received by email, fax or phone (all phone calls are recorded).

2. Goods are delivered and a goods received note is signed by the customer.

3. The goods received notes are kept in a file in the accounts office.

4. An invoice will be issued a few days after delivery on 30 day terms.

5. An aged analysis of trade debtors is produced monthly.

6. A reminder telephone call is made when the debt is 7 days overdue.

7. When a debt is 14 days overdue a letter is sent.

8. When the account is 28 days overdue the account will be put on stop.

9. The debt will either be placed in the hands of a debt collection company or legal proceedings could be instigated if the customer does not respond to calls or letters.

10. The business is credit insured, however insurance is only given for customers once they have a history of trade with the business of at least 12 months and have successfully paid for at least 3 invoiced amounts.

AGED DEBTOR ANALYSIS AS AT 31 MARCH 2010

	Balance	0 – 30 days	31 – 60 days	61 – 90 days	Over 90 days
	£	£	£	£	£
Customer					
A Limited	10,000	10,000			
Beckham & Co	25,000			25,000	
Cole Limited	60,000	30,000	30,000		
Dlay Limited	35,000	10,000	10,000	15,000	
F. Iddle Limited	60,000	60,000			
Gerard Limited	25,000	5,000	20,000		
Giggs Limited	10,000	(50,000)	10,000		50,000
G O Limited	25,000				25,000
Handover company	33,000	33,000			
Incase Limited	20,000			20,000	
Jo King Limited	120,000	30,000	30,000	30,000	30,000
New co limited	40,000	20,000	20,000		
S L Y Limited	99,200		44,200	55,000	
S Carpa Limited	100,000			100,000	
S ole Trader	3,000				3,000
X Soletrader	6,000			6,000	

TASKS

The assistant responsible for credit control has been on sick leave for several months but you have access to notes she prepared.

Notes provided by the assistant credit controller

a)   A Limited is a new customer and placed its first order a few weeks ago.

b)   Beckham & Co have said that they placed an order for a particular grade of product but received a different product and are therefore not prepared to pay the invoice.

c)   Cole Limited is a new customer and has said that a cheque is in the post. There is a rumour circulating that the company is having financial problems and has not been paying its suppliers. Cole Limited has placed an order for £10,000 of goods.

d)   Dlay Limited has a history of paying late but they have always paid eventually

e)   F. Iddle Limited is a long standing customer and has always settled their account within trading terms.

f)   Gerard Limited has gone into administration. The account is not credit insured.

g)   Giggs Limited sent a payment of £50,000 but did not provide details of which invoices the payment relates to.

h)   G O Limited is a new customer and has said that the goods were not received in good condition. The delivery note states that any claim for poor quality goods has to be notified to Alpha Limited within 24 hours. G O Limited only raised a problem with the goods when they were called for the second time. They did not mention that the goods were poor quality on the first call or within 24 hours of delivery.

i)   Handover Limited is a new customer and has only placed the one order. They have not responded to any correspondence and the letter was returned stating the company had gone away.

j)   Incase Limited is a new business and traded on cash with order. The assistant credit controller allowed the order to be processed before the cheque had cleared. The cheque subsequently bounced and the company is not returning calls.

k)   Jo King Limited is a long established customer and has always paid eventually, but has a history of late payments. The Managing Director of Jo King Limited is a personal friend of Alpha Limited's Managing Director.

l)   Newco Limited has been purchasing £20,000 per month

m)   SLY Limited is a regular customer and normally pays to terms.

n)   S Carpa Limited has recently gone into liquidation. S Carpa Limited had been a customer for 5 years and the account is credit insured.

o)   S ole trader is an individual customer who is refusing to pay even though there is no dispute.

p)   X Sole trader keeps saying that the cheque is in the post.

Required

Review the aged debtor analysis and the assistant's notes and prepare an action plan.

The action plan should include a summary of options available for the company to pursue and recommendations for provisions or write off of bad debts where appropriate.

ANSWERS

Section 1 – Online assessment

1.1	A	Offer, acceptance, consideration, intention to create legal relations and certainty of terms only
1.2	C	The promise to exchange value
1.3	D	Promising to pay for the pizza
1.4	C	The checkout assistant takes Dave's goods
1.5	D	An invitation to treat
1.6	B	Consideration
1.7	B	Michael's letter is an offer and John's response that he can supply the sugar is an acceptance
1.8	B	Misrepresentation
1.9	C	Suppliers to charge interest on overdue amounts owing
1.10	B	Harry cannot force Nita to pay the additional amount because the agreement was for £200.
2.1	A	Data about individuals only
2.2	A	All records held by the company
3.1	C	A Small Claims Court
3.2	A	There is a contract in existence and the non payment is a breach of contract
3.3	B	An action for price
3.4	C	The right of the seller to retain ownership of the goods until payment is made
3.5	B	£750
4.1	D	Liquidity management is important so that the company can ensure that cash is available to discharge commitments
4.2	B	i), ii) and iii) only
4.3	D	i), v) and vi) only
4.4	A	Aged creditor analysis

4.5   C   A rule that approximately 80% of the value of the amounts owed will be represented by approximately 20% of the customer accounts

5.1   B   To improve the cash flow of a business

5.2   A   £950, and 136.84%

6.1   B   A finance house lends money against invoices issued

6.2   A   Amounts owed by a customer who has defaulted on payment

6.3   D   Debt collection agencies get results because customers take more notice and are more likely to pay

Section 2 – Online Project

Part (a): X and Z Limited

X Limited Year	Indicator 2009	Rating	Indicator 2008	Rating
Operating profit margin	− 23.33%	− 5	− 8.18%	− 5
Interest cover	0	− 30	0	− 30
Current ratio	0.93	− 20	1.11	− 10
Gearing	48.78%	10	18.52%	20
		− 45		− 25

Z Limited Year	Indicator 2009	Rating	Indicator 2008	Rating
Operating profit margin	14.44%	10	6.88%	5
Interest cover	5.2	10	2,2	0
Current ratio	1.53	10	1.54	10
Gearing	47.17%	10	54.35%	0
		40		15

comments

X Limited achieves a high risk credit score and should therefore be turned down for a credit limit. A letter/note should be drafted explaining in a polite way the reasons for refusal of credit, and what the company could do to improve its chances of getting credit in future.

Z Limited achieved a low risk and therefore credit can be given.

Y Limited

| Y Limited | Indicator | Rating | Indicator | Rating |
Year	2009		2008	
Operating profit margin	6.92%	5	12.50%	10
Interest cover	0.9	– 20	3	0
Current ratio	1.24	– 10	1.18	– 10
Gearing	66.23%	– 20	43.48%	10
		– 45		10

The above table shows that Y limited's credit rating has reduced substantially and is now rated as a high risk. However, there are certain factors in its favour. These include:

- A good trading history over several years, although recently they have made some late payments.

- The expansion plan and the fact that the bank has given loans for the purchase of new assets is a good sign.

- New customers have ordered goods and have indicated that they will continue in 2010.

- The company is still liquid with cash at bank at the year end.

It is worth considering taking some kind of security over the business or personal guarantees from the directors or to consider retention of title clauses. There is no right decision and as long as the credit controller considers all the issues and makes a reasoned decision, credit will be awarded.

PART (b)

Students need to provide a reasoned argument for each overdue account, and recommend actions and provisions. For example: Gerard has gone into administration, which means that nobody can petition for liquidation. Alpha needs to consider retention of title claims, contacting the administrator, discussing further supplies (which will be guaranteed by the administrator), and registering a claim, which may result in a dividend.

Index

for your notes

for your notes

for your notes

for your notes

for your notes

for your notes

for your notes

for your notes